FRIENDS ON THE PATH

Dhamma reflections from
Ajahn Sundara and Ajahn Candasiri

Published for free distribution by
AMARAVATI PUBLICATIONS

This book is available for free download at
www.forestsanghapublications.org

Friends on the Path

Published by:

Amaravati Publications,
Amaravati Buddhist Monastery,
Great Gaddesden,
Hemel Hempstead,
Hertfordshire, HP1 3BZ
UK

Contact Amaravati Publications at www.amaravati.org
This book is available for free download at
www.forestsanghapublications.org

ISBN 978-1-870205-24-5

Cover photo by jchanders.

Leaf drawing by Emma Pettersson.

Produced with the LaTeX typesetting system. The body-text is typeset in Gentium,
distributed with the SIL Open Font Licence by SIL International.

First edition: 10,000 copies, printed in Malaysia – 2011

Printed in Malaysia by Sukhi Hotu.

*"Try to be mindful and let things take their natural course.
Then your mind will become still in any surroundings, like a
clear forest pool. All kinds of wonderful, rare animals will
come to drink at the pool, and you will clearly see the nature
of all things. You will see many strange and wonderful
things come and go, but you will be still.
This is the happiness of the Buddha."*

AJAHN CHAH

We would like to acknowledge the support
of many people in the preparation of this book,
and especially to the Kataññuta group of Malaysia, Singapore
and Australia, and the Sukhi Hotu Sdn Bhd group,
for bringing it into production.
shpj@sukhihotu.com

CONTENTS

Dedicated to the memory of our parents:

Jeanne & Jean-Emile Reynaud

Kathleen & Norman Cockburn

*and to all the other
wise teachers and friends
who have shown us the Way.*

INTRODUCTION

We have put together this small collection of writings in response to an invitation to reprint some of the nuns' published teachings. There being no collection of teachings that was considered to be suitable for re-printing in its entirety, we have gathered material from various sources.

The Buddha used the simile of the great ocean which has one taste – the taste of salt – to point out that all of the Teachings (Dhamma) and Way of Practice (Vinaya) that he presented in his lifetime are concerned with just one thing: freedom from suffering. In the same way, although the teachings that appear in this collection were given over a significant time span and in different situations, the single intention is to point to causes of suffering and to offer suggestions as to how these causes can be eliminated.

The title of the book, 'Friends on the Path', was chosen because it seems to be a theme in many of the teachings included here. We also recognize the central part that good friends (*kalyāṇamitta*) have played for each of us on our spiritual journey, and that the *Dhamma-Vinaya*, the teachings and the training of the mind and body presented by the Buddha can also be seen as good friends and supports on the Path of liberation from suffering. We have been sharing this journey for more than thirty years and our continuing friendship through the ups and downs, disagreements and challenges of monastic life could also be seen as a testament to the efficacy of the Buddha's teachings and way of practice.

We would like to acknowledge our debt of gratitude to our teacher, Ajahn Sumedho, for his total dedication and untiring energy in pointing out the way of freeing the heart.

May all beings be free,
Ajahn Sundara and Ajahn Candasiri

AJAHN SUNDARA is French and was born in a liberal non-religious family. After studying dance, she worked and taught for a few years in that field. In her early thirties she encountered the Dhamma through Ajahn Sumedho's teachings and a ten day retreat that he led in England. Her interest in Buddhist teachings grew, and in 1979 she joined monastic community of Chithurst Monastery where she was ordained as one of the first four women novices. In 1983 she was given the Going Forth as a *sīladhara* (ten precept nun) by Ajahn Sumedho. Since then she has participated in the establishment of the nuns' community, and for the last twenty years has taught and led meditation retreats in Europe and North America. As of 2011, she lives at Amaravati Buddhist Monastery.

AJAHN CANDASIRI is Scottish by birth and, like Ajahn Sundara, was one of the first nuns to be ordained by Ajahn Sumedho at Chithurst Monastery. Having been raised as a Christian, she continues to appreciate contact with contemplative Christians and with those of other faiths. Recognizing the immense benefit, both for herself and others, that can come about through a life of renunciation, she has actively participated in the evolution of the training and in providing opportunities for women to experience this form of practice. For most of her monastic life she has been resident at either Cittaviveka or Amaravati Monasteries.

1

WHY COME TO A MONASTERY?

Ajahn Candasiri

One question we all need to ask ourselves is, 'Why do we come to a monastery?' Whether we are monks, nuns, novices, lay guests or visitors, we should ask, 'Why have I come?' We need to be clear about this in order to derive the greatest benefit from what a monastery has to offer. If we are not clear, we can waste a lot of time doing things that may detract from the possible benefits to be found here.

The Buddha often spoke of three fires – three ailments – that we, as human beings, are afflicted by. These three things keep us continually moving, never able to rest or to be completely at ease. They are listed as greed, hatred and delusion (*lobha, dosa, moha*). He also, out of compassion, pointed out the antidote.

Actually, these fires are based on natural instincts. For

13

example, greed, or sensual desire is what enables humanity to survive, whether it be the desire for food or the sexual drive. Without sexual desire, none of us would be here now … and, of course, without hunger, which is the desire for food, we would not be inclined to take in the nourishment we need to maintain the body in a reasonable state of health. However, a difficulty arises when we lose touch with what is needed or necessary, and seek sensual gratification for its own sake.

Another kind of survival instinct is our response to danger. Either we turn around and attack something that is perceived as a threat to our physical survival, or we try to get away from it. This is the basis for *dosa* – hatred or aversion. Clearly, this also has an important place in nature, but again we have become confused, and what we frequently find ourselves defending is not so much the physical body but the sense of self: what we perceive ourselves to be, in relation to another.

The third fire, which follows on quite naturally from this, is delusion – *moha*. We don't really see clearly or understand how things are; we don't really understand what it is to be a human being. Instead, we tend to fix ourselves and each other as personalities, or 'selves'. However, in fact, these are just ideas or concepts that we measure against other concepts of who or what we *should* be. Then, if anyone comes along and challenges that 'self', it can invoke a strong reaction – we instinctively attack, defend or try to get away from the perceived threat. Really, it's a kind of madness, when you think about it.

Now, as I said before, the Buddha, having pointed out the nature of the disease, also presented the cure. This came in the form of simple teachings which can help us to live in a way that enables us to understand, and thereby free ourselves from these diseases; they also help us to avoid doing things that exacerbate them.

This brings me to what I would suggest is the best reason for coming to a monastery. It could be said that the best reason for coming to a monastery is because we want to free our hearts from disease, from the bonds of desire and confusion; and we recognize that what is presented here is the possibility of bringing this about. Of course, there could be many other reasons too: some people don't really know why they have come – they just feel attracted to the place.

So what is it about the monastery that is different from what happens outside it?

It is a place that reminds us of our aspiration and our potential. There are lovely images of the Buddha and his disciples, which seem to radiate a feeling of calm, ease and alertness. Also, here we find a community of monks and nuns who have decided to live following the lifestyle that the Buddha recommended for healing those diseases.

Having recognized that we are sick and that we need help, we begin to see that in fact the cure is in direct opposition to the ways of the world. We see that if we are to cure ourselves, we need first to understand the cause of the sickness – which is the attachment to desire. So we need to understand the three basic kinds of desire: to get, to get rid of and to exist and be a separate self – in order to free ourselves from the attachment to them. Instead of blindly following desires, we need to examine them closely.

The discipline we follow is based on precepts – simple guidelines outlining the practice of responsible living. These, used wisely, can engender a sense of dignity and self-respect. They restrain us from actions or speech that are harmful to ourselves or others. They also delineate a standard of simplicity or renunciation, whereby we ask: 'What do I really need?' instead of simply responding to the pressures of a materialistic society. But we may well wonder: 'How do precepts help us to *understand* desire?'

In a sense, what our monastic discipline offers is a strong container within which we can observe desire as it actually arises. We deliberately put ourselves into a form which prevents us from following all of our desires. This allows us to see desire itself, and to notice how it changes.

Normally, when we are caught up in the process of desire there is no sense of objectivity. We tend to be totally identified with the process itself so it is very difficult to observe or to do anything about it, other than be swept along by it.

For example, with lust or aversion we can see that these are natural energies or drives – which, in fact, everyone has. We are not saying that it's wrong to have sexual desire – or even to follow it, in appropriate circumstances – and we recognize that it is for a particular purpose, and that it will bring about a certain result.

As monks and nuns we have decided that we do not want

to have children. We also recognize that the pleasure of gratification is very fleeting, in relation to possible longer-term implications and responsibility. So we choose not to follow sexual desire. However, this does not mean that we don't experience it. It doesn't mean that as soon as we shave our heads and put on a robe, we immediately stop experiencing any kind of desire! In fact, what can happen is that our experience of these desires is enhanced when we come to a monastery. This is because in lay life we can do all kinds of things to make ourselves feel okay – usually without really being aware of what it is that we are doing. Sometimes there is just a subliminal sense of unease, followed by the reaching out to get something to relieve it – always moving from one thing to the next.

In the monastery it's not so easy to do this any more. We deliberately tie ourselves down – in order to look at the drives, energies or desires that would normally keep us moving. Now you might ask: but what kind of freedom is this, tying ourselves down in a situation where we are constantly restrained, always having to conform? Always having to behave in a particular way; to bow in a particular way, and at particular times; to chant at a particular speed and pitch; to sit in a particular place, beside particular people – I've been sitting next to or behind Sister Sundara for years! What kind of freedom is this?! It brings freedom from the bondage of desire. Rather than helplessly, blindly, being pulled along by our desire we are free to choose to act in ways that are appropriate, in harmony with those around us.

It's important to realize that 'freedom from desire' does not mean 'not having desire'. We could feel very guilty and really struggle if we thought like that. As I said before, desire is part of nature. The problem arises because it has been distorted through our conditioning: our education, upbringing, and the values of society. We are not going to get rid of it just like that – just because we want to, or feel that we shouldn't have desire. It's actually a more subtle approach that's required.

The monastic form and precepts can help us to make a peaceful space around the energies of desire so that, having arisen, they can burn themselves out. It is a process that takes great humility because first we have to acknowledge that the desire is there, and that can be very humbling. Often, particularly in monastic life, our desires may seem extremely petty; the sense of self may be bound up in things that seem very trivial. For example, we might have a very strong idea about how carrots should be chopped; then, if someone suggests we do it differently we can become very agitated and defensive! So we need to be very patient, very humble.

Fortunately, there are some simple reference points, or refuges, which can provide us with security and a sense of perspective amid the chaotic world of our desires. These of course are Buddha, Dhamma, Saṅgha: the Buddha, our teacher – also that within us which knows things as they are, seeing clearly, not confused or agitated by sense impression; the Dhamma, the teaching or the Truth, how things actually are right now – often quite different from our ideas about things; and Saṅgha – the lineage or community of those who practise, and also our aspiration to live in accordance with what we know to be true, rather than following all kinds of confused and selfish impulses that can arise. The Buddha gave some simple ways of turning to these. These are called the Four Foundations of Mindfulness.

Mindfulness of the body is one I use a great deal in my own practice. The body can be a very good friend to us – because it doesn't think! The mind, with its thoughts and concepts can always confuse us, but the body is very simple – we can notice how it is at any moment.

If someone acts or speaks in an intimidating way, I can notice my instinctual reaction, which is to tense up in a defensive attitude and perhaps respond aggressively. However, when I am mindful of the process, I can choose not to react in this way. Instead of breathing in, puffing myself up, I can concentrate on breathing out – relaxing, so that I become a less threatening presence to the other person. If, through mindfulness, I can let go of my defensive attitude they too can relax, rather than perpetuating the process of reactivity. In this way, we can bring a little peace into the world.

People visiting monasteries often comment on the peaceful atmosphere they find here. But this is not because everyone is feeling peaceful, or experiencing bliss and happiness continuously – they can be experiencing all kinds of things. One Sister said that she had never experienced such murderous rage or such powerful feelings of lust until she entered the Saṅgha! What is different in a monastery is the practice.

So whatever the monks and nuns might be going through, they are at least making the effort to be present with it, bearing it patiently, rather than feeling that it shouldn't be like that, or trying to make it change.

The monastic form provides a situation in which often renunciation and constraint are the very conditions for the arising of passionate feelings. However, there is also the reassuring presence of other samanas. When we're really going through it, we can speak to an older, more experienced Brother or Sister in the life, whose response is likely to be something like, 'Oh yes, don't worry about that; it will pass. That happened to me. It's normal, it's part of the process of purification. Be patient.' So we find the confidence to continue, even when everything seems to be collapsing or going crazy inside.

Coming to a monastery we find people who are willing to look at and understand the root cause of human ignorance, selfishness and all the abominable things that happen in the world; people who are willing to look into their own hearts, and to witness the greed and violence that others are so ready to criticize 'out there'. Through experiencing and knowing these things we learn how to make peace with them, right here in our own hearts, in order that they may come to cessation. Then, maybe, rather than simply reacting to the ignorance of humanity and adding to the confusion and violence that we see around us, we are able to act and speak with wisdom and compassion in ways that can help to bring a sense of ease and harmony among people.

So it's definitely not an escape, but an opportunity to turn around and face up to all the things we have tended to avoid in our lives. Through calmly and courageously acknowledging things as they are, we begin to free ourselves from the doubts, anxiety, fear, greed, hatred and all the rest which constantly bind us into conditioned reactions.

Here, we have the support of good friends, and a discipline and teachings to help keep us on course in what sometimes seems like an impossible endeavour!

May we all realize true freedom.

Evaṃ.

2

FREEDOM WITHIN RESTRAINT

Ajahn Sundara

When the Buddha taught the First Noble Truth, he said that taking refuge in human existence is an unsatisfactory experience. If one attaches to this mortal frame, one will suffer.

Not getting what you want is painful – that's quite easy to relate to. Getting what you don't want can also be painful. But as we walk a little further in the footsteps of the Buddha, even getting what we want is painful! This is the beginning of the path of awakening.

When we realize that getting what we want in the material world is unsatisfactory too, that's when we start to mature. We're not children any more, hoping to find happiness by getting what we want or running away from pain.

We live in a society that worships the gratification of desires. But there are many of us who are not interested so much in just gratifying desires, because we know intuitively that this is not what human existence is about. I remember many years ago when I was trying to understand what the Truth was, and I had no concept for it. I knew in a way that it was something beyond the reach of my thinking and emotional mind, something that transcended this world of birth and death.

As time went on, the desire to live a life that was truthful and real became the most important thing. As I was trying to harmonise my thoughts, my feelings and my aspirations and come to a place of peace, I became aware of the huge gap between my mind and my aspirations, what I would call 'myself', and this body with its five physical senses. At the time, I didn't even realize that the Buddhist teaching presented human beings with a sixth sense, the mind, the platform on which thoughts can arise.

Mind and body are a reservoir of energy and I found that my energy fluctuated, depending on how I used them. My way of relating to life and my understanding of it seemed also to be dependent on the clarity of my mind, and in turn that clarity was very much conditioned by the degree of energy I had. So I was quite keen to find out how to live without needlessly wasting that energy.

Many of us have not been raised up with a very disciplined life-style. In my family I was brought up within an atmosphere that fostered a certain amount of freedom of expression. Yet, following our whims and fancies, doing what we want, when we want, doesn't actually bring much wisdom to our life, nor much compassion or sensitivity. In fact, it makes us rather selfish.

Despite not having been inculcated with any great sense of discipline, as a child I appreciated the beauty of being alive, the harmony of life, and the importance of not wasting it. Yet the idea of living in a restrained and disciplined way was quite alien to my conditioning.

When I came across meditation and the practice of insight, it seemed a much easier introduction to discipline than following moral precepts or commandments. We often tend to look with alarm upon anything that is going to bind us, any convention that is going to limit our freedom. So most of us come to discipline through meditation. As we look into our hearts at the way we relate to the world of our senses, we come to see how everything is interconnected. Body and mind are constantly influencing and playing on each other.

We know well the pleasure involved in gratifying our senses when, for example, we listen to inspiring music or when we are looking at beautiful scenery. But notice how, as soon as we attach to the experience, that pleasure is spoiled. This can be very painful, and often we feel confused by the sensory world. But with mindfulness we gain insight into the transient nature of our sensory experiences, and become acquainted with the danger of holding on to something that is fleeting and changing. We realize how ridiculous it is to hang on to that which is changing. And with that realization we naturally recoil from wasting our energy on following that which we have little control over and whose nature it is to pass away.

Sense restraint is the natural outcome of our meditation practice. Understanding the danger of blindly following our senses, the desires connected with them, and the objects connected with the desires is one aspect of discipline. Understanding naturally brings about the application of this discipline. It is not sense restraint for its own sake but because we know that sense desires do not lead to peace, and cannot take us beyond the limitations of identification with our mind and body.

When we first come to live in the monastery we have to adopt the discipline of the Eight Precepts. The first Five Precepts point to what is called Right Action and Right Speech: refraining from killing, from stealing, from sexual misconduct, from lying and from taking drugs and intoxicants. The next three focus on renunciation, such as refraining from eating after a certain time, dancing, singing, playing musical instruments, beautifying oneself and from sleeping on a high and luxurious bed. Some of these precepts may sound irrelevant in our day and age. What do we call a high or luxurious bed today for example? How many of us have a four poster bed? Or why is dancing, singing or playing an instrument not allowed as a spiritual practice?

When we ordain as a nun or a monk, we take onboard even more precepts and learn to live with an even greater restraint. The relinquishment of money, for example, makes us physically totally dependent on others. These standards may sound very strange in a society that worships independence and material self-reliance. But those guidelines begin to make more sense when integrated into our meditation practice. They become a source of reflection and put us in touch with the spirit behind them. We find that they help us to refine our personal conduct and to develop a deep awareness of our physical and mental activity and of the way we relate to life. So that when we look into our hearts, we can see clearly the results and consequences of our actions by body, speech and mind.

Following such discipline slows us down, too, and requires that we be very patient with ourselves and others. We generally tend to be impatient beings. We like to get things right straight away, forgetting that much of our growth and development comes from accepting the fact that this human body and mind are far from perfect. For one thing, we have kamma, a past that we carry around with us which is very difficult to shed.

For example, when we contemplate the precept about refraining from incorrect speech, we have the opportunity to learn to not create more kamma with our words, and to prevent it from being another source of harm and suffering for ourselves or for other beings. Right speech (*sammā vācā*) is one of the most difficult precepts because our words can reveal our thoughts and put us in a vulnerable situation. As long as we are silent, it's not so difficult. We can even seem quite wise, until we start talking. Those of you who have been on retreats may remember dreading having to relate verbally again with human beings. It's so nice, isn't it, just to be silent with each other; there are no quarrels, no conflicts. Silence is a great peacemaker! When we start talking, it's another ball game.

We can't really fool ourselves any longer. We tend to identify strongly with what we think, and so our speech, the direct expression of thoughts, also becomes a problem. But unless we learn to speak more skilfully, our words will continue to be quite hurtful to ourselves and to others. Actually speech itself is not so much the problem but the place it comes from. When there is mindfulness, there are no traces left behind. Sometimes we say something that is not very skilful, and afterwards, we think how we could have said it better. But if we speak mindfully, at that moment somehow the stain of that self-image that is so powerfully embedded in us is removed or, at least, diminished. As you follow this path of practice, discipline really makes sense. When you begin to get in touch with the raw energy of your being, and the raw energy of anger, greed, stupidity, envy, jealousy, blind desires, pride, conceit, you become very grateful to have something that can contain it all. Just look at the state of our planet, Earth: it is a great reflection on the harmful result of a lack of discipline and containment of our greed, hatred and delusion.

So we need to be very mindful and careful to be able to contain our energy within the framework of a moral discipline, because our mind's deepest tendency is to forget itself. We forget ourselves and our lives' ultimate fulfilment, and instead fulfil ourselves with things that cannot truly satisfy or nourish our heart. This discipline also requires humility because, as long as we are immature and follow our impulses, we will feel repressed and inhibited by the discipline and, consequently, instead of being a source of freedom, we will feel trapped by it. We are very fortunate to have the chance to practise and realize that our actions, our speech or our desires are not ultimately what we are.

As our meditation deepens, the quality of impermanence of all things becomes clearer. We become more and more aware of the transient nature of our actions and speech, and our feelings related to these. We begin to get a sense for that which is always present in our experiences, yet is not touched by them. This quality of presence is always available and isn't really affected by our sensory interactions. When this quality of attention is cultivated and sustained we begin to relate more skilfully to our energy, to our sense contact and the sensory world. We discover that mindful attention is actually a form of protection. Without it, we're simply at the mercy of our thoughts or our desires, and get blinded by them. This refuge of awareness and the cultivation of restraint protect us from falling into painful hellish states of mind.

Another aspect of discipline is the wise attention and wise use of the material world. Our immediate contact with the physical world is through the body. When we learn how to take care of the physical world, we are looking after the roots of our lives. We do what is necessary to bring the body and mind into harmony. This is the natural outcome of restraint. Slowly, we become like a beautiful lotus flower that represents purity and grows out of the water while being nourished by its roots in the mud. You may have noticed how the Buddha is often depicted sitting on a lotus flower which symbolises the purity of the human heart. Unless we create that foundation of morality rooted in the world of our everyday life, we can't really rise up or grow like the lotus flower. We just wither.

In monastic life, the skilful use of the Four Requisites – clothes, food, shelter and medicine – is a daily reflection which is extremely useful because the mind is intent on forgetting, misinterpreting or taking things for granted. These four requisites are an essential part of our life. It is a duty for us monastics to care of our robes. We have to mend them, repair them, wash them and remind ourselves that we only have one set of them and that these robes have come to us through the generosity of others. The same goes for the food that we eat. We live on almsfood. Every day people offer us a meal because we are not allowed to store food for ourselves for the next day. So our daily reflection before the meal reminds us that we can't eat without thinking carefully about this gift of food. As alms mendicants, we also reflect on the place we live in. You may not like the wallpaper of your room, but the reflection on our shelter: 'this room is only a roof over our head for one night' helps us to keep our physical needs in perspective. We consider also that without the offerings of these requisites we could not lead this life. This reflection nurtures a sense of gratitude in the heart.

Taking care of the physical world and what surrounds us is an essential part of the training of mind and body and of our practice of Dhamma. If we are not able to look after that which is immediate to us, how can we pretend to take care of the ultimate truths? If we don't learn to tidy our room every day, how can we deal with the complexities of our mind?

To reflect on simple things is very important, such as looking after our living place, and not misusing our material possessions. Naturally it is more difficult to do this when we have control over the material world and can use money to buy what we want, because we easily get careless, thinking: 'Oh well I have lost this' or 'I have broken that, never mind, I'll get another one.'

Another aspect of discipline and restraint is Right Livelihood. For a monk or a nun, there is a long list of things we should not get involved with, such as fortune-telling or participating in political activities, and so on. I can appreciate the value of this more and more as I see how, in some parts of the world where the Saṅgha has got involved in worldly issues, monks find themselves owning luxurious items or even becoming wealthy landlords. Right Livelihood is one aspect of the Noble Eightfold Path which covers a wide range of activities such as not deceiving, not persuading, hinting, belittling or bartering, and not involving ourselves in trades of weapons, living beings, meat, liquor, or poisons.

These guidelines call for a careful consideration of how we want to spend our life, and what kind of profession or situation we want to get involved in. The reflections on the precepts, the requisites, Right Livelihood and the discipline of our mind and body are the supportive conditions within which the ultimate discipline can manifest in our hearts. That ultimate discipline is our total dedication to the Truth, to the Dhamma, and the constant aspiration of our human heart to go beyond our self-centred lives. Sometimes we can't really say what it is, but through the practice of meditation we can be truly in touch with that reality, the Dhamma within ourselves. All spiritual paths and spiritual disciplines are here as supportive conditions and means for keeping alive this aspiration to realize Truth in our heart. That's really their aim.

3

A QUESTION OF BALANCE

Ajahn Candasiri

Every winter at our monasteries two or three months are set aside as quiet retreat time – a time to focus more intensively on our inner work. The encouragement given during this time is towards cultivating a stiller, quieter space within the heart. For it is only through attention to this that we are able to observe all our skilful and less skilful habits, and to train the mind – making it into a good friend, a good servant, rather than an enemy that can lead us into all kinds of unhappiness.

Emerging from such a period of retreat highlights a dilemma faced by many people – whether living as householders, or in a monastic environment. The question it poses regards finding an appropriate balance between essential 'inner work' – which requires periods of withdrawal and seclusion – and our relationship with 'the world', including

the responsibilities we have within our respective communit-
ies (whether family, or monastic Saṅgha) and towards the
greater whole. If our attention and energies are directed only
outwards towards our spiritual companions or towards society, it becomes clear sooner or later that even if we expend
every ounce of energy right up until the last breath, there
will still be more to do. The needs, the suffering of the world
'out there' is endless. We can never make it *all* all right. If we
try, as many of us have to do before the penny finally drops,
the result can be exhaustion, despair and disillusionment.

Eventually we see that actually it's a question of balance.
We need to find a way of balancing our 'inner' work and our
'outer' work – and we begin to appreciate a basic paradox:
that in order to be truly generous, truly of service to others,
we actually need to be completely 'self-centred'. We need
to be able to stay in touch with our own hearts, listening
carefully to what they tell us, even while engaged in external
activity or interaction. We need to remain attentive to our
own needs, and to really make sure that these are well taken
care of – even if it means disappointing people, letting them
down, not living up to the expectations they may have of us
(or that we have of ourselves). This is not at all easy, with the
conditioning most of us have: 'Don't be selfish'.

There is a simile given by the Buddha of two acrobats.
The master said to his pupil, 'You watch out for me, and I
will watch out for you. That way we'll show off our skill successfully and receive our reward.' But the pupil contradicted
him, 'But that won't do at all, Master. You should look after

yourself, and I'll look after myself ... *that* is how we shall perform successfully!' The Buddha then goes on to explain that, in a sense, it was the pupil who had got it right. Watching out for ourselves through the practice of mindfulness – really applying ourselves to cultivating of the Four Foundations of Mindfulness – benefits others ... and being mindful in regard to others is a way of taking care of our own hearts. Furthermore, we care for others through patience, gentleness and kindly consideration; this also is a way of protecting our own hearts.

During his lifetime, the Buddha established the Fourfold Assembly[*] as a social structure that would facilitate the cultivation and maintenance of the qualities of mindfulness and consideration of others. However – whether we go forth as monks or nuns or live as householders – one thing is clear: it's likely to take time. This practice has to be developed and worked at over a lifetime.

Usually, things don't just change and fall into place with the first glimmer of insight. We need to do the work of laying the foundation, using the tools and guidance that the Buddha presented. Even though these were presented over 2,500 years ago they still work well, having been used over generations by men and women to shape their lives – to enable the ripening of the potential that each one of us has. It waits quietly in the heart for us to choose to make its cultivation the priority of our lives.

---

[*]*Fourfold Assembly*: The community of monks, nuns, laymen and laywomen.

4

FEARLESS PRESENCE

Ajahn Sundara

The Buddhist path is a path of training the heart and mind: educating the heart to recognize Dhamma when it is present and when it's not. It is a path that leads to a greater sense of happiness, well-being, and confidence. It deepens our human experience and its gracefulness.

And yet, many of us practise for years and still find ourselves frustrated, feeling that we aren't going anywhere, not getting the results that we expect. We are not happy. We wonder why a path that is supposed to lead us to happiness and peace does not seem to do the job.

We often have expectations about the way things are and the way things should be. We have expectations about life, practice, and the results that we should get. How many of us are really willing to simply be aware and present with the mind, here and now, and see it clearly as it is? Isn't that what the teaching is constantly pointing to? The cultivation of awareness, the development of wisdom, and the Four Foundations of Mindfulness are all teachings pointing to being in the here and now, and from this perspective, clearly seeing the nature and content of the mind.

The training of the heart is about awareness of the simplicity of the present moment. It is refreshing and freeing to be awake and to be content where we are and with what we have. Yet, while a part of us loves to be at peace, another loves excitement. One part is really happy to let go of the ego mechanisms, while another would rather die than let go. A part of us loves the idea of letting go when things are difficult, but another part can be quite terrified of liberation.

The Buddha foresaw this difficulty and put suffering at the centre of his teaching. When we meditate and are mindful of suffering, we can see its impermanence and feel motivated to free ourselves from it. The Buddha's teaching is for those who have seen the suffering of delusion. Delusion is a misperception of reality. Do we really experience ourselves as we are? Or do we experience ourselves as we wish to be?

We are reminded to be present, to be here and now but we easily get bored with that. We think, 'Well, I have been in the here and now for years, and nothing seems to have changed much.' We mistake the path of practice with the path of making our life more interesting or becoming a happier person. We don't realize that this path is a path of liberation from ignorance. It can take us down avenues that are not necessarily comfortable. The journey of transformation and liberation is not a comfortable one – it goes against the grain, it disturbs the status quo. Are we ready for that? Or are we just satisfied with being a little happier in relationships: with our mother, our partner, our job, and our lifestyle. Do we simply hope to make the conditioned world a bit more comfortable?

It is not wrong to wish for better conditions of life, because all sentient beings wish for happiness. The Buddha never said that happiness was wrong. But his teaching points to a type of happiness that is unshakeable, one that is not dependent on neurotic and obsessive desires. It is the happiness that comes from the realization of the end of suffering, and that leads us to a deeper confidence and true freedom. This means that no matter what happens to you in life, this happiness cannot be taken away from you. Isn't it wonderful? You can be old, sick, you may not be getting what you want, you may be in pain, you may be criticized, treated unfairly and yet, instead of being miserable, your mind remains happy. That is what the Buddha points to and the way that he teaches.

Things can change but our heart ceases being dependent for its happiness on anything external, on any worldly things, or on what people think about us. People can think that we are stupid, but we know ourselves well enough that it's okay for them to think what they want to think. It's okay for your mother to see you as a failure, or for your partner to think that you are no good. People have the right to think the way they want and you have the same right. We don't need to agree or feel victimized, undermined or crushed with what the world is doing to us. This is what the Buddha's teaching is aimed at, an inner independence of the heart which brings true compassion.

Are we ready for this path of awakening? Are we ready for this journey? Or are we still waiting for some kind of saviour to take us by the hand and tell us, 'Okay my dear, everything is going to be fine. You'll be able to smell the flowers from the beginning of the path till the end. It will be lovely – beautiful sky, lovely mountains, everybody will love you, your mind will be blissful and peaceful, and I promise you that it will be like that forever.'

Well, the truth is that if you want to really live in the present moment, you have to be fierce. And what I mean by fierce is that sometimes what you are aware of may be sweet, but actually witnessing the delusion of the mind is not particularly sweet.

Māra is the personification of that which is called evil in Buddhism. Māra's presence is found throughout the Buddha's life story and his teachings. Māra is that which distracts us from the present moment, robbing us of clarity, insight, peace and sanity. Yet, Māra is nothing more than our deluded self! A Sufi teacher once said, 'If you want to know where the devil is, just look at yourself.' No need to go very far – if you want to find Māra just check out your comfort zones.

So, are we ready to walk this path? Are we ready to be awake?

A great chunk of our practice is about building a strong

container that can withstand the power of our difficult experiences – from this vulnerable, open, awakened state, building a refuge in which we can abide comfortably. The first step is what the Buddha calls *sīla*, or ethics. Many of you know the Five Precepts of not harming, not stealing, not taking anything that doesn't belong to you, not abusing anybody else or yourself with your own sexuality or sensuality, not speaking in ways that are harmful, and not taking drugs or intoxicants that confuse your consciousness. Those precepts can be just formulas that we repeat by rote every week, or they can be pointers for reflection to build a more peaceful abiding in ourselves. Why? Because you may have noticed that every time we break any ethical standards, we experience a lot of regret and unhappiness.

Why is it not easy to enter this path? Because sometimes it's like going into a battle – waging a war between our worldly mind and the awakening heart, the Dhamma heart. It is not necessary to create a duality between the world and the heart, but the actual experience of seeing both levels is often felt like that – conflicting energy, opposed desires. And this is what I mean when I talk about going into battle. We don't have to go into battle all the time, but on the path we have to face many desires that are not in line with *sīla* or what we truly, deeply wish for ourselves.

How much room do we give to the Dhamma that is blossoming and strengthening in our own being, and how much room do we give to our ignorance and self-concerned desires? We want to be kind, loving, caring and patient but many of our habits are contrary to this. We find ourselves struggling, full of aversion, impatient, demanding, and critical.

This path does not require that we surrender ourselves to some kind of higher entity who is going to work magic tricks on us. This path does not ask you to call upon some kind of divine intervention. It is a path that transforms our heart through our own effort and endeavour. Taking the Three Refuges actually does that to a degree. Whenever we take the Three Refuges and really bow inwardly to the Three Refuges – Buddha, Dhamma, Saṅgha – that symbolises the awakening heart in yourself; the Buddha, the truth of the teaching of the Buddha, and those who have liberated themselves. Each time we take refuge in something that is vaster than our little mind. Instead of taking refuge in 'me', 'mine', what upsets 'me', what is self-obsessive, I take refuge in my awakened heart, in the truth within myself that opens my heart and mind to the bigger picture.

Have you noticed how when we look at ourselves we keep bumping into our obstacles? That is why the practice can feel quite frustrating sometimes if we don't have somebody experienced who can explain to us that obstacles are actually okay. Feeling wretched, undermined, miserable, and all that sort of thing is fine because these are only states of mind, perceptions that are impermanent.

Naturally, the backdrop of those things is not always clear. That is why mindfulness is cultivated, because it's the backdrop. Sometimes, those things are very deeply rooted in our mind. It's not easy to uproot them and let go of them.

Sometimes it may take years of witnessing particular patterns or particular responses to life before being free of them. Everything in you knows not to hold on to them, yet we have other emotional aspects that are preventing the process of letting go. But we have enough knowledge and understanding to realize that although our mind may be feeling stuck, a great chunk of ourselves is not stuck at all and feels fine.

To be able to turn around and take refuge in the bit that is not stuck is an art and a skill. On this spiritual path we are able to keep looking at the part of ourselves that is already free, and take refuge in that. Of course, we need all the help we can get. It is very fortunate to have a good teacher such as Ajahn Sumedho to whom I can go to for advice, and who is not necessarily going to pamper me or tell me how good I am but who can remind me to stay mindful, wakeful, and very present with things that may be quite difficult, or even unbearable.

Whatever arises in the mind, just don't cling to it. If you do this often enough with whatever arises, with difficulties and problems, it really works. Something shifts and is transformed. Your world changes and as your mind gains more and more confidence in the realm of Dhamma, the Truth. It loses its trust in your desires and fears.

A lot of our inability to let go comes from fear. We are frightened of letting go of things because everything we know, even our miseries, is comforting on an emotional level – it's better than not knowing. Ajahn Sumedho taught us for many years to train the mind to face the unknown, and when questions arise just say, 'I don't know ... I don't know ... I don't know.' Training the mind just like that.

Do that in your everyday life. Allow the Dhamma to inform your consciousness, rather than continuing on the treadmill of the conditioned mind's activities. All the conditioned mind can do is to go from one thought to another. It's not that there is something wrong with the thinking mind. The thinking mind is useful for contemplation, for reflection, for clarification and living your everyday life. As you contemplate the space of your mind, you can look at thoughts not as belief systems, but just as energy, as images, forms. Then you can make clear what it is you want to consciously think, and what you don't want to think.

The path of practice is divided into three aspects; *sīla* or ethics, *samādhi* or the practice of meditation that includes effort or energy, concentration, and mindfulness, and *paññā*, or wisdom – Right Understanding and Right Intention.

This practice leads to a lot of joy, happiness, and peace. But as long as it is dependent on something, it is going to change. So we can't count on something that depends on impermanent causes. This practice is leading you to understand a mind that is in many ways very treacherous and tricky. To relate to ourselves and to our mind in a sound, sane, kind, and patient way in the face of this trickiness and delusion is a real skill. It's a training, it's an education, it's something we do little by little. It doesn't come by itself. We must learn to really take care of our actions – body and speech and mind.

Most of us start with the mind. We get interested in meditation and then notice how angry we can get, or we notice the *kilesas*, the afflictive emotions, or unskilful mental states that are very unpleasant. Then, we notice our attachment. Even being attached to being a good person is painful because it is going to blind you. There are a *lot* of elements in ourselves that are blinding. We unravel these things when we are ready to open ourselves to our life fully, fearlessly. You can only do this if your goal is very clear. If you reflect on why you started on this path in the first place and what you want to do with it, or whether you really want to be free, you would be surprised to hear that perhaps you don't want to be free and that you just want your piece of cake and to eat it! Hearing that voice is enough. You don't have to believe it because it's not you.

At some point, you have to be very clear that this path of practice is for the sole purpose of freeing the heart from misery, *dukkha*. So, when you experience *dukkha* don't shy away from it because this is your opportunity. It's not a problem, it's your opportunity to liberate your mind from its attachment to ignorance. It's what you are supposed to see.

I leave you with this.

5

JESUS WITH BUDDHIST EYES

Ajahn Candasiri

His Holiness, the Dalai Lama, speaking to a capacity audience in the Albert Hall in 1984 united his listeners instantly with one simple statement: 'All beings want to be happy; they want to avoid pain and suffering.' I was impressed at how he was able to touch what we share as human beings. He affirmed our common humanity, without in any way dismissing the obvious differences.

When invited to look at 'Jesus through Buddhist eyes', I had imagined that I would use a 'compare and contrast' approach, rather like a school essay. I was brought up as a Christian and turned to Buddhism in my early thirties, so of course I have ideas about both traditions: the one I grew up in and turned aside from, and the one I adopted and continue to practise within. But after re-reading some of the gospel stories, I would like to meet Jesus again with fresh eyes, and to examine the extent to which he and the Buddha are in fact offering the same guidance, even though the traditions of Christianity and Buddhism can on the surface appear to be rather different.

To start with, let me say a little about how I came to be a Buddhist nun.

Having tried with sincerity to approach my Christian journey in a way that was meaningful within the context of everyday life, I had reached a point of deep weariness and despair. I was weary with the apparent complexity of it all. Despair had arisen because I was not able to find any way of working with the less helpful states that would creep, unbidden, into the mind: the worry, jealousy, grumpiness, and so on. Even positive states that could turn around, and transform themselves into pride or conceit – which were of course equally unwanted.

Eventually, I met Ajahn Sumedho, an American-born Buddhist monk, who had just arrived in England after training for ten years in Thailand. His teacher was Ajahn Chah, a Thai monk of the Forest Tradition who, in spite of little formal education, won the hearts of many thousands of people, including a significant number of Westerners. I attended a ten day retreat at Oakenholt Buddhist Centre, near Oxford, and sat in agony on a mat on the floor of the draughty meditation hall, along with about forty other retreatants of different shapes and sizes. In front of us was Ajahn Sumedho, who presented the teachings and guided us in meditation, together with three other monks.

This was a turning point for me. Although the whole experience was extremely tough – both physically and emotionally – I felt hugely encouraged. The teachings were presented in a wonderfully accessible style, and just seemed like ordinary common sense. It didn't occur to me that it was 'Buddhism'. Also, they were immensely practical and as if to prove it, we had, directly in front of us, the professionals – people who had made a commitment to living them out, twenty-four hours a day. I was totally fascinated by those monks: by their robes and shaven heads, and by what I heard of their renunciant lifestyle, with its 227 rules of training. I also saw that they were relaxed and happy – perhaps that was the most remarkable, and indeed slightly puzzling, thing about them.

I felt deeply drawn by the teachings, and by the Truth they were pointing to: the acknowledgement that, yes, this life is inherently unsatisfactory, we experience suffering or dis-ease – but there is a Way that can lead us to the ending of this suffering. Also, although the idea was quite shocking to me, I saw within myself the awakening of interest in being part of a monastic community.

So now, after more than twenty years as a Buddhist nun, what do I find as I encounter Jesus in the gospel stories?

Well, I have to say that he comes across as being much more human than I remember. Although there is much said about him being the Son of God, somehow that doesn't seem nearly as significant to me as the fact that he is a person: a man of great presence, enormous energy and compassion, and significant psychic abilities. He also has a great gift for conveying spiritual truth in the form of images, using the most everyday things to illustrate points he wishes to make: bread, fields, corn, salt, children, trees. People don't always understand at once, but are left with an image to ponder. Also he has a mission – to re-open the Way to eternal life; and he's quite uncompromising in his commitment to, as he puts it, 'carrying out his Father's will.'

His ministry is short but eventful. When I am reading through Mark's account, I feel tired as I imagine the relentless demands on his time and energy. It's a relief to find the occasional reference to him having time alone or with his immediate disciples, and to read how, like us, he at times needs to rest. A story I like very much is of how, after a strenuous day of giving teachings to a vast crowd, he is sound asleep in the boat that is taking them across the sea. His calm, in response to the violent storm that arises as he is sleeping, I find most helpful when things are turbulent in my own life.

I feel very caught up in the drama of it all; there is one thing after another. People listen to him, love what he has to say (or in some cases are disturbed or angered by it) and are healed. They can't have enough of what he has to share with them. I'm touched by his response to the 4,000 people who, having spent three days with him in the desert listening to his teaching, are tired and hungry. Realising this, he uses his gifts to manifest bread and fish for them all to eat.

Jesus dies as a young man. His ministry begins when he is thirty (I would be interested to know more of the spiritual training he undoubtedly received before then), and ends abruptly when he is only thirty-three. Fortunately, before the crucifixion he is able to instruct his immediate disciples in a simple ritual whereby they can re-affirm their link with him and each other (I refer, of course, to the Last Supper) – thereby providing a central focus of devotion and renewal for his followers, right up to the present time.

I have the impression that he is not particularly interested in converting people to his way of thinking. Rather it's a case of teaching those who are ready. Interestingly, often the people who seek him out come from quite depraved or lowly backgrounds. It is quite clear to Jesus that purity is a quality of the heart, not something that comes from unquestioning adherence to a set of rules. His response to the Pharisees when they criticize his disciples for failing to observe the rules of purity around eating expresses this perfectly: 'There is nothing from outside that can defile a man' – and to his disciples he is quite explicit in what happens to food once it has been consumed ... 'rather, it is from within the heart that defilements arise.' Unfortunately, he doesn't at this point, go on to explain what to do about these.

What we hear of his last hours: the trial, the taunting, the agony and humiliation of being stripped naked and nailed to a cross to die – is an extraordinary account of patient endurance, willingness to bear the unbearable, without any sense of blame or ill will. It reminds me of a simile used by the Buddha to demonstrate the quality of *mettā*, or kindliness, he expected of his disciples: 'Even if robbers were to attack you and saw off your limbs one by one, should you give way to anger, you would not be following my advice.' A tall order, but one that clearly Jesus fulfils to perfection: 'Father, forgive them for they know not what they do.'

So why did I need to look elsewhere for guidance? Was it simply that Jesus himself was in some way lacking as a spiritual template? Was it dissatisfaction with the Church and its institutional forms – what Christianity has done to Jesus? Or was it simply that another way presented itself that more adequately fulfiled my need at that time?

Well, in Buddhism I found what was lacking in my Christian experience. It could be summed up in one word: confidence. I don't think I had fully realized how hopeless it had all seemed, until the means and the encouragement were there. There is a story of a Brahmin student called Dhotaka, who implored the Buddha: 'Please, Master, free me from confusion!' The Buddha's perhaps somewhat surprising response was: 'It is not in my practice to free anyone from confusion. When you yourself have understood the Dhamma, the Truth, then you will find freedom.' What an empowerment!

In the Gospels we hear that Jesus speaks with authority; he speaks too of the need to have the attitude of a little child. Now, although this could be interpreted as fostering a child-like dependence on the teacher, Buddhist teachings have enabled me to see this differently. The word, 'Buddha', means 'awake' – awake to the Dhamma, or Truth, which the Buddha likened to an ancient overgrown path that he had simply rediscovered. His teaching points to that Path: it's here, now, right beneath our feet – but sometimes our minds are so full of ideas about life that we are prevented from actually tasting life itself!

On one occasion a young mother, Kisagotami, goes to the Buddha, crazy with grief over the death of her baby son. The Buddha's response to her distress, as she asks him to heal the child, is to ask her to bring him a mustard seed – from a house where no one has ever died. Eventually, after days of searching, Kisagotami's anguish is calmed; she understands that she is not alone in her suffering – death and bereavement are inevitable facts of human existence. Jesus, too, sometimes teaches in this way. When a crowd had gathered, ready to stone to death a woman accused of adultery, he invites anyone who is without sin to hurl the first boulder. One by one they turn away; having looked into their own hearts, they are shamed by this simple statement.

In practice, I have found the process to be one of attuning, of attending carefully to what is happening within – sensing when there is ease, harmony; knowing also when one's view is at odds with What Is. I find that the images that Jesus uses to describe the Kingdom of Heaven explain this well. He says it is like a seed that under favourable conditions germinates and grows into a tree. We ourselves create the conditions that either promote well-being and the growth of understanding, or cause harm to ourselves or others. We don't need a God to consign us to the nether regions of some hell realm if we are foolish or selfish – it happens naturally. Similarly, when we fill our lives with goodness, we feel happy – that's a heavenly state.

On that first Buddhist retreat it was pointed out that there is a Way between; neither following, nor struggling to repress harmful thoughts that arise. I learned that, through meditation, I can simply bear witness to them, and allow them to pass on according to their nature – I don't need to identify with them in any way at all. The teaching of Jesus that even to have a lustful thought is the same as committing adultery had seemed too hard; while the idea of cutting off a hand or foot, or plucking out an eye should they offend makes logical sense – but how on earth are we to do that in practice? I can see that it would require far more faith than I, at that time, had at my disposal! So I was overjoyed to learn of an alternative response to the states of greed, hatred or delusion that arise in consciousness, obscure our vision, and lead to all kinds of trouble.

As the Dalai Lama said, 'Everyone wants to be happy; no one wants to suffer.' Jesus and the Buddha are extraordinary friends and teachers. They can show us the Way, but we can't rely on them to make us happy, or to take away our suffering. That is up to us.

6

THE KNOWING MIND

Ajahn Sundara

In this practice we develop that quality of mind which knows – the 'knowing' mind. Not 'reacting' mind, but the 'knowing' mind. It's very different. Within the quality of knowing you can see everything. You can see the reactions. You can see the pain. You can see the joy. You can see the peace. You witness everything.

This knowing does not fight what's going on, or try to change what's going on, or make something out of what's going on. As we make peace with everything that is happening now, the quality of knowing can strengthen itself, enabling you to clearly mirror what is going on. The knowing mind can mirror everything that's happening. This is the path of knowledge, the path of knowing, the path of understanding.

Know change. Know that comfort and discomfort, pleasure and pain, succeed each other naturally. You don't need to pick them up all the time. Just know that much. When there is a pleasant, comfortable, bright mind, you know that certain conditions have brought this about. The opposite is true too – when there is discomfort and confusion in the mind, other conditions have brought this about. *You* haven't done it. It just *happens*. You think *you* do it, but actually, this is just the Dhamma, this is just nature. And if you stop picking up this high and low, pleasure and pain cycle, the mind settles down and becomes more peaceful. Peace and happiness don't come from picking up one side of reality and avoiding the other. Peace and happiness come from not picking up anything at all.

Let go. As you sit, the mind that knows is powerful. This is the power of the knowing, the capacity of the knowing, the breath of the knowing mind, this is our refuge. This is what we call 'The Buddha Refuge', the One Who Knows.

Just be the witness of what you are. It doesn't seem like much, but it's completely transformative. It's like comforting an old friend who has been in trouble – not mistreating him or her. We bring loving-kindness to the experience of this mind, this body, this person here who may be struggling or confused about what is going on with their life. Make peace with this old friend.

The knowing mind is not necessarily an experience that we are familiar with. The experience of the six senses is a familiar experience. When you say 'hot and cold', 'pleasant', 'lovely', 'delightful', 'delicious', you know what it means. There's a kind of familiarity about our sensory world that is relatively easy to pin down. But the knowing mind is a strange thing. You can't put your finger on it. It has a mirror-like quality – a 'witness' quality that enables you to know yourself and to know the nature of your mind and body.

The Buddha's teaching helps us investigate the nature of mind and body in the light of three characteristics – *anicca, dukkha, anattā* (impermanence, pain or suffering, and not-self). These are very abstract concepts at first, but as you begin to bring the knowing mind into your experience it becomes utterly obvious. Pain comes and goes. Qualities of the mind such as happiness, dullness, expansiveness, tightness, and concentration, come and go. This is what you need to look at carefully in your meditation – to see change. It's a learning process. Learn to see *dukkha* as a direct experience, not as a conceptual perception.

Learn, also, to see *anattā*, not-self, as a direct experience. Notice that *you* don't have much control over what you are experiencing. Whatever arises passes away and is not really under your ownership. You don't own this mind and body. If you owned your mind you could tell it to do this or do that, and it would do it. 'Don't be miserable!' and you would not be miserable. 'Wake up!' and you would wake up.

Although we don't have control over what we experience, there is still a certain amount of decision that we can make. We can decide to sit upright, and to be attentive – we can *intend*. Intention is very powerful, so there is some element of intention. You can *intend*, but things might not happen the way you expect, or the way you imagine, or the way you anticipate. You just *intend*. You decide to be awake this morning – maybe you will, maybe you won't. That's okay. Just still be the witness. Sometimes you are awake. Sometimes you are asleep. At least your intention is very clear. You can make it clear. This is as much as you can do, just intend, and then witness the result of that intention.

Intention is very powerful, especially in the morning when the mind is still very malleable, soft, not yet caught up in all the wilfulness of worldly pressures. That's why people say it's very important to sit in the morning and prepare your heart and mind for this day. One doesn't often realize the importance of starting the day with a clear intention to see the way things are, to acknowledge what's happening in ourselves, and to do what we have to do, no matter whether we feel lazy, or we feel elated, inspired, or dispirited. If there is something we need to do, we just do it.

Maybe you have a hard time getting up in the morning. Just make that conscious. Maybe you are a night owl and you prefer waking up late, you find early mornings difficult. You don't need to fit your mind's image of the perfect Buddhist meditator – just witness the struggle of your mind, or the discomfort. If your mind is bright and comfortable in the morning then notice that too. The more you witness and take refuge in the knowing mind, the more you will find that whatever needs to be discarded will be discarded. Whatever is not useful will just naturally fall away, but not through rejection or aversion – simply through the knowing of this experience in each moment.

The knowing mind will enable you to remove obstacles. As you continue your meditation practice and get in touch directly with the three characteristics of existence, you will gain confidence in another whole reality of yourself which is not dependent on attachment and fear and blind desires. This is the fruit of the Dhamma practice; strengthening the refuge of knowing, strengthening the awakened mind, strengthening our confidence and trust in the mind that knows. The more you trust it, the more you will experience that life goes on much better without an identity, a self, an attachment to *dukkha*, and an ignorance of *anicca*. Life goes on much better with knowing impermanence, knowing pain for what it is and letting go of the habitual tendency to think you are in charge. And as you practise, trust increases – trusting in the Dhamma, trusting in the knowing, trusting in your intention.

In the world, we need to keep our intentions clear. We need to use thoughts and develop clarity of intention. The power of our mind doesn't lie in attaching to habits. The power of our mind comes from letting go of fear, from letting go of delusion, and increasing clarity. Let go of control, let go of habits, and take on board the power of clarity that makes you intend things in the right directions. Intend things so that you increase the happiness in your life. Intend to develop that which is good and refrain from doing evil. By intending with clarity, the development of the mind becomes a vital, essential practice.

7

ME FIRST

Ajahn Candasiri

This evening I would like to talk about the *Brahma Vihāras.* These are states that arise quite naturally when the mind is free from self-interest. They are the lovely boundless qualities of *mettā* – kindliness, *karuṇā* – compassion, *muditā* – sympathetic joy, or gladness at the beauty, the good fortune of others, and *upekkhā* – equanimity, or serenity. I really like this teaching because even though, mostly, we are nowhere near that level of pure radiance, they are qualities that we can bring forth in smaller ways.

Over the years my understanding of them has altered quite radically. I used to try radiating kindness out to others, having compassion for others, delighting in the good fortune of others and finding equanimity in the midst of suffering – but I could never really do it, it never seemed to work very well. When I was trying to be glad at the good fortune of others, all I could feel was jealous. When I was trying to feel equanimous about the suffering around me, all I could feel was disturbed and upset. When I tried to feel compassion, all I could feel was anxiety: 'What can I do to make it all right?' When I was trying to feel kindness towards people I didn't like very much and it didn't work, I used to just hate myself. I became thoroughly confused, so I realized that I had to try a different approach.

I remember when I first told people that I was going to be a nun, one immediate response was, 'Well, how selfish! Isn't that awfully self-centred?' My reply was, 'Yes. It's completely self-centred ... but until I can understand my own suffering, my own difficulty, I'm not going to be able to help anybody else very much.' Although I wanted to help, I saw that my capacity for serving others was very limited and that, really, I had to begin here.

We can easily talk about world peace and about caring for others, but actually cultivating loving-kindness demands a lot. It demands a broadening of the heart and our view of the world. For example, I've noticed that I can be very picky about things. There are some things that I can feel boundless kindness and love for – but only as long as they are agreeable, and behaving in the way that I want them to behave! Even with people we love dearly, if they say something that is upsetting, a bit jarring, that channel of limitless, boundless love can close immediately; not to mention with the people that we don't like, or who might have different views from our own.

So it does take a bit of reflection to begin to broaden that sphere of *mettā*, loving kindness. We may manage to do it in an idealistic, intellectual way; we may find we can spread *mettā* to people we don't know or that we don't have to associate with, but that is very different from doing it with those we live with all the time. Then, it's not always so easy – much as we may want to. This can be a source of anguish: 'I really want to like this person – but they drive me nuts!' I'm sure you have all experienced this with certain people. You may even feel sorry for them – but they still drive you nuts! You can end up feeling that you *should* love them, but somehow you just can't. I have found Ajahn Sumedho's interpretation of *mettā* very helpful; he would say: 'Well, to expect to *love* somebody is maybe asking too much – but at least refrain from nurturing thoughts of negativity and ill-will towards them.' So, for me, the starting point for cultivating *mettā* has been simply the recognition of its absence, or even the presence of its opposite.

For many years I had a kind of subliminal negativity going on; quietly grumbling away, usually about myself: 'You're not good enough. You've been meditating all these years, and still your mind wanders and you fall asleep. You're *never* going to be any good.' – those kinds of voices. Are they familiar ... just quietly there, mumbling away, undermining any sense of well-being? It took me a long time to recognize how much negativity I was harbouring in my heart.

Then there can be grumbling about other people: 'Look at the way she sits!', 'Good heavens, he eats an awful lot!',

'I really don't like the routine of this retreat. Why do we have to get up so early?' You'll all have your own niggles. The important thing is not *not* to have them, but to recognize them – to actually allow ourselves to be fully conscious of this grumbling, negative mind; and then to be *very* careful not to add to the negativity by being negative about it: 'I never realized what a terribly negative person I am. I'm a hopeless case!' That's not very helpful. Instead, we can begin to take a kindly interest: 'Well, that's interesting. Fancy thinking like that; I never realized how much that mattered to me,' rather than hating ourselves for having such thoughts.

One thing I've discovered is that often the things I find hardest to accept in others are things that I actually do myself. It can be quite humbling, but incredibly helpful, to notice what others do or say that is upsetting. Then to ask inwardly, 'Is that something that I do?' Sometimes it can be difficult and painful to acknowledge but, fortunately, it can be a private process – we don't have to tell anyone else! Then, as we begin to soften and find that capacity for accepting ourselves – including all the foolishness, the inadequacy, the shyness – the heart expands, and we are able to extend acceptance and kindness towards a much greater range of people and situations. So this quality of *mettā*, of kindliness, has to start with this being here. We don't need to manufacture it, it arises quite naturally as we cultivate more kindliness and acceptance of ourselves.

This may seem strange if we have always been told we should think of others before ourselves but I have found that, in fact, trying to do it the other way round never really works. I might be able to do and say the right kinds of things, but often there'd be some quite harsh underlying judgement. For example, before I was sick, I used to feel critical of people who couldn't work as hard as I could. I'd say to them, 'Yes, do be careful; do rest if you need to,' but I'd be thinking, 'You're just so feeble; if you were practising correctly you'd be able to do it!' It was only after experiencing a state where, after ten minutes of work I'd need to rest for half an hour, that I really knew what that was like. Only then was I able to feel genuine kindness towards those in difficulty, or physically limited in some way.

As monastics, we make a commitment to harmlessness. However, the way our training works is to allow us to see directly those energies that maybe aren't so harmless, and aren't so beautiful: the powerful lust, sensuality or rage – they all come bubbling up. It can be rather alarming at first but now, having experienced those energies within my own heart, I can understand much better the state of the world and the things that happen in it. Of course, I can't approve of many of the things I hear about, but there is much less tendency to judge or to blame.

Karuṇā – compassion – is the second *Brahma Vihāra*. Looking at the word, 'compassion': '-passion means 'to feel', and 'com-' is 'with', so it's a 'feeling with', or entering into suffering. Now one response, when confronted with a situation of pain or difficulty, can be to distance oneself. It may come from fear – a feeling of, 'I'm glad that's not happening to me,' so we do and say the right kinds of things but, actually, there's a standing back and a sense of awkwardness about what we are feeling. This is what can happen. It reminds me again of when I broke my back. There was one person who was very uncomfortable about it; when we met I could sense that she was shocked, and that she didn't want to get too close. But for me, her response brought quite a lonely feeling; it didn't really hit the spot. So *karuṇā* implies a willingness to actually take on board the suffering of another, to enter into it with them. It's a much fuller kind of engagement and demands an attunement with one's own heart; having compassion for one's own fear or awkwardness around another person's situation.

Sometimes we feel awkward because we don't know what to say. If someone is bereaved or terminally ill, what do you say to them? We might be afraid of saying the wrong thing. However, when we are willing to be with our own sense of discomfort with the situation – to bear with our own pain or suffering in relation to it – we begin to sense the possibility of responding in a spontaneous, natural way.

This state of being fully present with another person in their difficulty is something that I trust now – much more than any *ideas* about a compassionate response. It's not about giving advice, or sharing the story of our aunt who had the same difficulty, or anything other than the willingness to be with the discomfort of the situation, to be with our own struggle. When we are fully present with suffering we find a place of ease, of non-suffering, and somehow we just know what is needed. It may be that nothing is needed, other than to be there; or perhaps something needs to be said, and suddenly we find ourselves saying just the right thing; or there may be some practical assistance we can offer. But none of this can happen until we have fully acknowledged our own struggle with what's happening. It needn't take more than a micro-second. We simply begin with tuning in to our own suffering, attending to that – from this arises the compassionate response to the other.

Muditā is the quality of sympathetic joy. This one has always interested me greatly – mostly because it was something that I often seemed to lack. I used to suffer enormously from jealousy, and there seemed to be nothing I could do about it. It would just come, and the more I tried to disguise it the worse it would get. I could really spoil things for people, just through this horrible thing that used to happen when I had a sense that somebody was in some way more fortunate or better than I was.

Considering the three characteristics of existence (impermanence, unsatisfactoriness, and lacking in any permanent self-hood) was what brought a glimmer of hope – to realize that jealousy is impermanent. Before, it would feel very, very permanent – as though I would have to do something extremely major to get rid of it, to make it go away. It also felt like a very personal flaw. So this teaching enabled me to recognize that this was just a passing condition – and that I didn't have to identify with it. It came, and it went. Certainly, it was extremely unpleasant – but when I could let go of the struggle for things to be otherwise, it actually didn't stay very long; it would come and it would go, and that would be it.

People used to tell me about their *muditā* practice. They'd say: 'Well, if I see somebody who has something better than me, I just feel really glad they have it' – but I hadn't quite got to that point, I must say – I didn't have such generosity of heart. I realized that there was still something missing. Eventually, I realized that what was lacking was *muditā* for myself. I realized that it was no good trying to have *muditā* for somebody else if what they had was something that I really wanted – and thought I hadn't got!

So I saw that, rather than lamenting my own lack (which is basically what jealousy is, and which I would find so painful to acknowledge) I had to begin to look at what I had, to count my own blessings. This may sound a little strange in a context where many of us have been encouraged to rejoice in the goodness and beauty of others, but where the last thing we are supposed to do is to count our own blessings, or to think of how good we are ... but I saw that that was actually what I needed to do.

I'm sure that everyone here can find some things to feel glad about. Even if there are not very many things we can make much of the few, rather than pushing them to one side, saying: 'No, they don't really count, that's nothing really – but look at all these terrible faults I have!' We are very good at doing that – but how good are we at looking at the goodness, the beauty of our lives? Everyone here can count the fact that they've chosen to come to the monastery, that there is a sincere interest in cultivating peace, as something to feel very glad about – particularly seeing how many people are living their lives. We can also make much of the things we do well. Instead of, 'Oh no, that wasn't very good,' we can try saying, 'Well, actually, that was rather a beautiful thing that I did. I did do that well.'

One person I know keeps a special diary. Whenever he does something good, he notes it in his diary. Then, when he is feeling a bit miserable, he reads it through – then he feels much better! That struck me as really skilful – a way of making much of goodness. Why not? Generally, we make so much of our misery and our inadequacy, why not instead try making much of the goodness of our lives? I began practising with this some time ago, and the more I've done it, the more naturally and spontaneously I can really feel happy when I hear of somebody else's success. Interesting, isn't it, how it works? So this is something I encourage you to contemplate: filling the heart with a sense of the beauty and goodness of *your* life, as well as that of others. Then, when people are having a really joyful time together, instead of sort of sneering and looking down on them – and feeling a bit lonely and isolated – we can join in with appreciation, sharing in their delight. That is *muditā*.

Upekkhā, equanimity, is the fourth *Brahma Vihāra*. To me, it seems significant that the Buddha made so much of this quality. Sometimes this is translated as 'indifference'; it's considered to be one of the highest spiritual states. Personally, I can't imagine that he would make much of 'indifference', the way we often use this word – a kind of not wanting to be bothered. So it's helpful to consider what this quality of equanimity, or serenity, actually feels like. What does it involve, in terms of the heart? One of the ways that I reflect now on *upekkhā* is to see it as a grandness of heart whereby there is the willingness to touch and be in contact with it all – from the most delightful state, to the most utterly wretched state. Having taken this human form, we are subject to wonderful, sublime experiences and, equally, to horrible, hellish miserable states. We can experience every realm of existence.

It's said that when the Buddha was dying, along with human beings, there were a great many *devatas* (heavenly beings) gathered around as well. Those who weren't enlightened were tearing their hair, weeping, in a state of great anguish: 'Oh no, he's dying, he's leaving us.' Whereas, the enlightened ones maintained perfect equanimity. They simply said: 'It's in the nature of things to arise and to cease.' They acknowledged that things were happening according to their nature: having been born, things die. I think we've still got a bit of work to do there!

Upekkhā implies an ability to stay steady amid the highs and lows of our existence – amid the eight worldly winds: praise and blame, fame and insignificance, happiness and suffering, gain and loss – these things that can affect us so much. When we contemplate life we see that sometimes things are good, and we feel great – sometimes they're horrible. This is normal; we all have horrible times. Knowing that things change deepens our capacity to stay steady with them, instead of being completely thrown when they don't work out so well.

In our community (as in any family) there are times when it's wonderful; we all get along really well together. This is just fine, we can enjoy those times; but there are also days when it's horrible. In an international community it's easy for people to misunderstand each other, and sometimes there can be a tiff. Having experienced a great number of difficult times over the years, I'm now usually able to stay much more steady. It's still unpleasant, but there isn't such a strong reaction – I don't feel that anything has gone terribly wrong. I've noticed too that somehow that capacity to stay steady helps everybody else to not be so badly thrown by what's happening. Whereas, when everybody is thrown, the whole thing escalates – then, it really does get out of control!

Reflecting on the law of kamma, we see that everything happens as the result of what has gone before. So instead of blaming ourselves, or looking around for someone else to blame when things seem to go wrong, we can simply ask, 'What is the lesson here? How can I work with this?' We can reflect that this is the result of kamma, and determine to maintain mindfulness; holding steady, rather than making the situation worse by some unskilful reaction. In this way we bring balance, not just into our own lives but for everyone else too. It's not such an easy thing but again, it comes back to acknowledging and making peace with our own sense of agitation, our own lack of equanimity.

Sometimes we come into contact with suffering that

seems almost unbearable. When this happens I've noticed a tendency to try to protect myself, to try to shut out such impressions. But *upekkhā* implies a willingness to expand the heart and to listen, even when things seem unbearable. As we practise, what seems to happen is that – far from becoming indifferent – we become able to encompass an ever-increasing range of experience; to be touched by life, as by a rich tapestry of infinite colour and texture. So it's definitely not a dumbing down or deadening, but rather an attunement to the totality of this human predicament. At the same time, we find an increasing capacity to hold steady with it: the balance of *upekkhā*. Through establishing ourselves in the present, and holding steady – whatever we might be experiencing – we find the resources for dealing with *whatever* we may encounter in this adventure we call 'life'.

Evam.

8

SIMPLICITY

Ajahn Sundara

The time I spent in Thailand practising meditation quite intensively was a great learning experience. For nearly two and a half years it gave me the chance to be part of a culture that was incredibly different from ours in its outlook on life; it also provided an environment that made me realize how much my mind was conditioned by Western values, assumptions, prejudices and conceit.

At first, many aspects of that culture were totally alien to me. There were so many things that I found impossible to understand; but by the time I left, I felt quite at home. So I would like to share with you some facets of the time spent in this beautiful country.

In the rural area where the monastery is located the people are mostly farmers, simple people, living uncomplicated lives. Unlike us, they do not seem to be burdened with a lot of psychological concerns or existential crises. Their lives revolve around immediate needs such as food, sleep, getting through the day, and simple pleasures of life. Thai people are great at enjoying themselves!

When I first met my teacher, Ajahn Anan, he asked me how my practice was going. I said that one of my interests in coming to Thailand was to have the opportunity to continue to develop it. Then he asked me if I had any difficulties, so I explained to him how I had been practising and how I was feeling about it at the time. It was quite extraordinary, as I was talking, suddenly to sense that I had a strong mirror in front of me, and to see this 'Me', going through its usual programme with clever justifications, suddenly turn into a big cloud of proliferation! This was a wonderful insight. With anybody else I might have been offended or felt that I had not been taken seriously but somehow, with him – maybe because he was just himself and deeply at ease – there was a huge sense of relief.

The way Thai people approach the teaching and themselves is deeply influenced by the Buddhist teaching and its psychology. Even their everyday language is mixed with many Pāḷi words. I remember noticing how their way of speaking about the mind/heart could seem quite cold-hearted to us. If you were going through some great suffering, some fear or painful memories, the teacher could just say: 'Well, it's just *kilesa* (unwholesome mental states).' Or, 'Your heart is not happy?'

Strangely enough, in that context such statements would completely deflate the habit to think in terms of 'Me' having a huge problem that needs to be sorted out. And there was always a strong and compassionate mirror and reflection. If anyone else had reduced my 'problems' to a simple feeling of unhappiness I would have been really annoyed and felt dismissed but, with Ajahn Anan, in whom I had a deep trust, I was able to see the way my mind worked and, when there was confusion, to drop it. I would be reminded of the present moment by the question: 'What's going on? Is your heart unhappy?' Of course, in the immediacy of the moment nothing was going on because the monastery, located in a lovely forest on the side of a mountain, had a very peaceful atmosphere. It was a simple place, quiet and secluded, and there was nothing to do all day except receive alms food, eat and sweep one's path for about half an hour. That was all. The rest of the time was free to develop formal practice. My mind calmed down a lot.

These experiences gave me a real taste for simplicity, and for the mind in its state of normality – the mind that does not create problems out of the way things are. I'm not saying that this seemingly simple and direct approach to the mind is right or wrong, but I found that practising in this environment and culture over a period of two years had a powerful effect. It helped me to stop the habit of creating myself as a person – and this was quite a liberating thing. As the mind calmed down I could see the person, the sense of 'Self', really clearly every time it arose.

The teaching pointed out that if we suffer through the sense of Self, we can't actually go very far in our practice; insight cannot arise deeply enough to cut off attachment. The whole culture facilitates this approach. If one thinks too much, people consider that one is on the verge of madness. Ask any Thai: when someone thinks too much, they'll say that she or he has a 'hot heart' – and if you are 'hot' ('*ron*', in Thai), you're seen as deluded. To have '*ronchai*' (hot heart) is quite negative, even insulting. People there are not much into thinking – I am not saying that it is good or bad but they don't trust the thinking mind. This was very different from the culture I came from where thinking is worshipped, tons of books are written, and people rely on and trust the intellect a lot. So it was interesting to be in a culture that functioned so differently – so much more intuitive, more feminine.

What struck me most when I came back to Europe was the complexity of the Western way of life, and I could see that having access to many traditions and teachers had turned our society on the spiritual level into a vast supermarket. This is not all negative, but it's extremely challenging for the mind that is already struggling with all it receives through the senses. No wonder people become neurotic after being exposed to so much information and so many choices!

When you're in the forest out there, you're just with a few birds, a few creepy-crawlies and nature all around. Days come, rise, and pass away with nothing much happening, and you get used to a very simple, peaceful rhythm. I found that extremely pleasant, and I knew that it was conducive to deepening the practice. In fact, I felt quite at home and very privileged to have that opportunity. The culture itself being predominantly Buddhist keeps things simple, the whole atmosphere was not one in which you felt intellectually stimulated; it's quite amazing the effect that this has on the mind. It would naturally slow down a lot, and become quite still. So I was scared to come back to the West and whenever I thought of coming back, my mind would conjure up the image of drowning in a huge ocean of thought – not a terribly auspicious sign!

Even though I had to adapt and to follow the Thai mae-chee etiquette, 'the Thai nuns' choreography', as I used to call it: walking in line to receive my food behind very young boys, crouching down every time I spoke to a monk – it was little, compared to the blessings and support I received there.

So I was not sure that I would cope with the life and rhythm of Amaravati. I decided that if I had to teach, I would keep things simple; I would just speak about practice, just facts: *ānāpānasati*, the five khandhas, or Dependent Origination. I would not complicate people's lives with more words, concepts and ideas.

But it was a great lesson in letting go when, a few weeks ago, I went to teach at a Buddhist group. As I was being driven there, I said innocently to the leader of the group: 'How do you see the weekend?' Of course, I already had some ideas: 'I'll just meditate with them. I'll really teach them how to do it, rather than to think about it – then we can share our experience afterwards.' But the person answered: 'Well, Sister, we really want to talk with you about practice, and ask you questions, and have some discussion on Dhamma, and ...' I thought, 'Oh dear! Never mind.' I just had to let go. I was reminded of the teaching of Luang Por Sumedho: 'Just receive life as it is. Don't make a problem about it. Open yourself to the way things are.'

Thai people do not seem to suffer much from self-hatred; they don't even seem to know what it means! Once, out of curiosity, I asked an educated Thai woman who had come to visit me: 'Do you ever dislike yourself?' And she said, 'No, never.' I was amazed. She had just been talking to me about some very painful issues in her life yet she was not critical. Self-negativity does not seem to be part of their psychological make up, whereas we are riddled with it. So we have a difficult beginning, because the first step on this path is to have peace in one's heart – which doesn't happen if there is a lot of self-hatred.

Fortunately Ajahn Sumedho, who is well acquainted with the Western mind, has devised a very good way of dealing with its tendency to dwell on the negative side of things and be critical – just recognizing it, and receiving it within a peaceful space of acceptance, love and ease. This is a mature step as most of us find it very difficult to create a space around experience, we tend to absorb into what comes through our minds and to create a Self around it.

Let's say we experience boredom; if there is no mindfulness, we easily absorb into that feeling and become somebody who is bored, somebody who has got a problem with boredom and needs to fix it. This approach hugely complicates a simple experience like boredom. So all we need to do is to allow space inwardly to contemplate that feeling, instead of fixing it as a problem. In Thailand where psychology and the Buddhist teaching are so intertwined, Ajahn Anan would simply say: 'Well it's just one of the hindrances.' Simple, isn't it? But often for us it can't be just an ordinary boredom – it's got to be a very personal and special one!

One of the things that attracted me most to the Buddhist teaching was the simplicity of its approach – I think this is what all of us would like to nurture in our practice and in our lives. The Buddha said: 'Just look at yourself. Who are you? What do you think you are? Take a look at your eyes and at visual objects. How do you receive that experience of sense contact? What are the eyes, nose, tongue, body and ears? What are thoughts?' He asks us to inquire into sensory experience, rather than absorb into it and react to pain and pleasure. He said to just observe and actually see the nature of experience, very simply, directly, without fuss. Just bring peacefulness and calm into your heart, and take a look.

The sensory experience is really what creates our world. Without knowing its source and its effect, it's very difficult to get out of the vicious circle of 'Me' and 'my problem' that needs to be sorted out, or 'Me, who loves it' – this kind of push and pull agitates the heart further. So instead of pushing and pulling we take a good look and, without getting involved, we know things as they are: impermanent, unsatisfactory, not self. But this requires certain conditions, it doesn't happen by itself.

The first condition is peace and calm; without that, it's very difficult to see anything. That's why a lot of our practice is actually to bring the heart to a state of balance and calm. Most people are in a constant state of reactivity. If you ask them if they suffer, they say, 'No'. They think they are perfectly fine. But someone who has seen the suffering of reactivity gradually comes to realize that it's not the best way to relate to life; it is very limited – always the experience of 'Self', 'Me' and 'You'. But as the sense of 'Self' decreases, the reactivity decreases, too.

It is not so much the sense of Self that is the obstacle, it's our identification with it. The Four Noble Truths point to that very experience: the suffering of attachment to Self, the belief that one has a permanent ego. One teacher gave the example of Self being like a necklace; when the beads are held together by a thread it becomes a necklace, but as soon as the thread is cut, the whole thing falls apart.

I've spent many years observing closely the experience of the sense of Self. I remember in the early days when I was upset, Ajahn Sumedho would say to me: 'Well you don't need to suffer about that. You've got the Refuges and …' – but this used to enrage me: 'But what about Me? I'm suffering right now!' I felt he was just dismissing the huge personal problem, and wasn't taking me seriously. So for years I cherished that sense of Self without knowing it. I didn't think I was deluded, no, I was simply taking myself seriously!

In Thailand if you suffer and talk about it, you quickly get this funny sense that your practice has gone down the drain. This may be because in the quiet and simple life of a forest monastery, the formal practice is strongly rooted in the development of concentration, *samādhi*. It's a different approach there.

At Amaravati, the foundation of our practice is the Four Noble Truths which point again and again to suffering, its cause, its relinquishment and the path. It's not so easy here to get refined states of mind because we are constantly impinged upon by sense contacts: things, work, many strong-minded people living together, etc. Ajahn Sumedho teaches that to free the mind one just needs to put this teaching into practice right until the day we die.

I was struck by how soft and gentle the psyche of the Thai people is compared to ours; I found them generally very easy going. They like to laugh a lot, and basically life is no problem; if you make one you are considered kind of stupid. Even very simple villagers will think that if you make a problem out of life you are stupid. This was a nice contrast to our tendency to complicate life, and create problems around most things – mainly because we have not been taught a better way. Our whole culture is based on the view that the world is understood through the thinking apparatus, rather than through the silent knowing, the awakened mind.

For our practice to bear fruit it's important to not make too much of ourselves. Basically, as long as we are fascinated by ourselves we will be bound to suffering. When the mind is undermined by streams of self-centred thoughts such as: 'I don't like myself', 'I think I've got a problem', and so on, it ends up being fed the wrong food, filled with unskilful states (*akusala dhamma*). The realization of Dhamma is dependent also on the strength of our mind, so how can that come about if there is not a certain degree of positive energy? That's why *mettā*, kindness and acceptance, is very important. We don't get a bright mind by filling it with a lot of negative states; that weakens it. Whether it's anger, greed, jealousy or despair, if their true nature is not seen they weaken the *citta*, the heart. But when we see them in the light of mindfulness, then they have no power over us. Try meditating filling your heart with *mettā*, then with miseries and then with joy – you'll see the difference, it's quite simple. You can do the same with anger; bring up things that make you angry for a moment and see how it affects the heart. These are just conditioned mental states, but often we are not really aware of how they affect us; this is the work of delusion.

So knowing very clearly the difference between what is skilful and unskilful, not from an intellectual point of view but from wisdom, is great progress. The Buddha's teaching is like a map that helps us to recognize skilful and unskilful dhammas which we should learn to recognise and let go.

Remember, your heart is like a container filled with things that come from the past. If we've been a thief, or lazy or arrogant, or loving and generous in the past then we'll have certain habits. When we meditate, we receive the result of our habits – we can't just throw them away at will. Wouldn't it be nice if we could? We'd all have been enlightened a long time ago! So bearing patiently and compassionately with one's kamma is very important.

One thing that has become clearer from my experience in Thailand is that while the actual practice is always here and now, it's also a gradual process, like developing a skill. It needs concentration, mindfulness and effort. They are the tools needed to gain insight into our attachments and to let them go. We're all here to liberate the heart from delusion, to learn how to live free from remorse or confusion. For the fruits of practice to arise in the heart, we need to develop these qualities of mind.

Here in the West we make a big deal about the body, and demand a lot from it. It's got to be healthy, strong and comfortable; whereas, in the East, it's made much less of. It's important of course, as without it we would not be able to practise but if it cracks up or deteriorates, there is no need to agitate the mind. So as meditators, if we talk too much about our body, or want to sleep a little bit more, we are basically considered a lousy practitioner! From a Buddhist perspective, it is the mind that is more important, since it will condition what happens when you die. When the mind is strong and healthy, then the body calms down naturally, and benefits a lot more than when we allow ourselves to be overwhelmed by concern for its well-being. This outlook gave me a more balanced perspective on the physical body, and a more detached way to deal with it. The mind can easily dwell upon negative aspects of oneself or other people. This is the easiest way of looking at life; the hardest thing is to actually train the heart to follow the path of goodness, *kusala dhamma*, skilful dhamma. We may feel down or depressed but consider, it's only one mental state, one moment; do we want to perpetuate such a state for a lifetime? Or can we actually, through wisdom, realize that it's only one moment, one feeling, one thought? Such realization brings a real sense of urgency. If we are going to have feelings, or to think – which we can't avoid – we might as well guide our mind towards things that are skilful. Anything else just drags us down to hell, but actually we do this to ourselves quite a lot unknowingly.

So we have an option: we can stay in hell, the realm of miseries, or in heaven, the realm of happiness, or we can stay in a state of peace that comes from wisdom – knowing that when pleasant feelings, pleasant experiences are present, that's heaven and when it's unpleasant, that's hell. The moment you know both as they are, that's freedom, isn't it? The mind doesn't linger – that's the middle way. We can't control life and it takes time to go beyond wanting heaven or fearing hell. Just the way people walk or open doors, the way they speak or eat can send you to hell or heaven. It doesn't take much. Isn't that ridiculous? Sometimes we feel blissed out or we feel friendly to the whole universe, then, coming back to our dwelling place we find somebody's making a bit of noise, and suddenly we feel enraged. It doesn't take much, does it? So life is very unstable. Yet there is the knowing, that moment of freedom when you know: 'Ah, this is a feeling, sense contact, ear, nose ... '

The teaching of the Buddha, remember, is to know sense contact, its object and the effect it has on the heart. So we hear our neighbours making a lot of noise: 'I'm going to tell them off, I can't stand it!' But when we are able to let go of it, we notice that we don't mind really ... but then the noise starts again, and finally we find ourselves in front of their door knocking: 'Can you stop it!' And of course, if there is no wisdom at that moment, no mindfulness, then later on, we feel remorseful: 'I feel awful, I shouldn't have done that.' and the whole cycle of suffering starts again.

The path shown by the Buddha is very simple. We need to remind ourselves again and again to have *sati*, mindfulness. It's like an endless refrain: *sati, sati, sati*. Where are we now? The practice of awareness is always in the present moment. There's no knowing in the future or the past. We can know a thought that takes us into the past or the future, but in the moment there is just knowing, awareness.

We can remind ourselves that we are all here to train and keep the practice simple. To know what nurtures the heart: truth, peace, calm, compassion, *mettā*. When we have *mettā*, the ego, the Self, can dissolve. Notice how when people have *mettā* for us, peace arises in our heart, doesn't it? When people feel love towards us, we feel more peaceful and more calm. This is what we can do for ourselves too, and if all of us do this with one another, it will be a good basis for the practice.

I just want to leave you with this: let's keep things very simple and remind ourselves that whatever complicates life, it's not something to trust. It's more likely to be the work of my friend Māra, the Self or ego. When the heart is at peace and there is understanding, then things are quite cool, quite peaceful, quite okay. So I wish you to cultivate kindness and infinite patience towards yourself, and towards whatever resultant kamma you have to work through and that may be bothering you at this time. This is why the Buddha said that patience and endurance are the highest disciplines.

9

TAKING REFUGE

Ajahn Sundara

After three or four days on a meditation retreat we tend to look a lot brighter and happier than when the retreat began. This is the natural outcome of looking inwardly and being present with what is happening in ourselves. However horrible things might feel, as we listen closely to our heart and mind some lovely things happen, we begin to relax. It's not easy, yet we begin to be more accepting of all the pain, of the suffering that we usually tend to put aside. We never seem to have the time and the space to live in harmony with ourselves. So when we go on retreat what a wonderful opportunity to be able to listen, and perhaps to understand a bit more profoundly the nature of our mind, the nature of our thoughts, of our feelings and perceptions. We have the chance now to realize that we only feel limited and bound by them because we rarely have the opportunity to pay attention to, or investigate and question their reality.

Before giving a talk, we traditionally take refuges in the Buddha, the Dhamma and the Saṅgha. When we become a monastic, a homeless one, we trade our home and we get Three Refuges. So we're not totally homeless. We actually take three very secure refuges and we leave behind all that we suppose to be safe, that we assume to be protective and secure. We leave behind home, family, money, the control of our lives, the control over the people we live with, the place we actually stay – we let go of all that. And in return, we take the Three Refuges.

Now, in my experience these refuges did not mean very much at first. I didn't quite understand what they were about. Several times a year, we have Buddhist festivals and ceremonies. We follow a lovely custom on those days. We meditate through the night and before the all-night vigil we slowly walk around the monastery three times holding a candle, some incense and some flowers in our hands. Monastics and lay people walk together silently around the monastery contemplating the Three Refuges; the Buddha, the Dhamma, and the Saṅgha. It's a very beautiful and inspiring sight. At first I didn't know what this really meant. I knew somehow that those refuges were in the human heart and perhaps as I practised I would come to know what they meant. I felt at that moment that I had a whole lifetime to understand this, so I just relaxed considering that the Buddha, Dhamma, Saṅgha wasn't something I had to think about.

I think what brings many of us to be interested in the practice of meditation is the need to understand ourselves, the need to clarify the confusion we live in. Many of us want to be free; we want to understand and see for ourselves what this life is all about. At some point we get fed up with books; we've read enough, we've listened enough, we've met enough wise people. We've done everything we could to understand, and yet that didn't seem to be sufficient. Second-hand knowledge somehow is not really satisfactory. We want to experience for ourselves what all these wise people and all the wise teachings are saying. As long as there's no realization of the nature of our mind there's no real understanding. It's difficult to taste the joy and the freedom of knowing and experiencing the Buddha's teaching for oneself – what's known as insight, seeing directly into the nature of our mind and body and realizing the freedom experienced when we let go of any attachments. At the beginning of the path of practice we still tend to look for a form of happiness. We all want to be happy, don't we? Who wants to be miserable? We all want to feel free and to experience pleasure.

The practice is not here to make us suffer. We only suffer because we haven't practised properly yet, we haven't done what is necessary to let go of ignorance, to let go of our attachments. So it's important to take this into account. We should not imagine that because we are practising we have to be terribly serious and feel that unless we experience some terrible pain or hardship that somehow something is not quite right. But more often than not it's true that, unless it hurts, our ignorance is not acknowledged. If it doesn't hurt, we can go on forever without really being aware of it. This seems to be our human predicament. Unless something hurts, we don't really wake up, we don't open our eyes and look. So everyday we recite the Three Refuges as a reminder, because out of habit we tend to take refuge in things like anger and worry, self-pity, pleasure and distraction. So our tendency is to take refuge in the wrong things, things that make us unhappy. And if we didn't have reminders, if we didn't have skilful means to bring back into consciousness what's really important in life, we would forget ourselves and never see the way out of suffering.

REFUGE IN THE BUDDHA

The refuge in the Buddha is the refuge in the knowing. The Buddha knows the world – which in Buddhism does not mean the world of mountains, rivers and trees, but the world that arises in our mind and body, and the suffering that we create out of ignorance. In our daily chanting we say that the Buddha knows the world, he knows the arising of the world, the ending of the world, he knows the way the mind creates the realities we live in and through taking refuge in mindfulness, in the 'one who knows', we begin to see clearly the path that leads us out of suffering.

Somebody was asking me today, 'Who is the one who knows? Who is the one who is aware?' A good question, isn't it? Because I have never found anybody 'who knows', have you? I tried for a long time and finally gave up, and ever since I have made peace with the fact that there is nobody who knows. Just knowing. Knowing seems to be able to carry on functioning with or without my doubts. Without having an answer, I can still take refuge in being the 'knower', being the one who's aware, who can see. The 'One who knows' is that factor that balances out the extremes of the mind. We can see the extremes of the mind, happiness, unhappiness, pleasure and pain, inspiration and despair. We can see hope and depression. We can see praise and blame. We can see agitation, sleepiness, boredom, the whole lot. And that seeing is a balancing factor, because we become aware of our attachments to these moods, these states of mind. Without a refuge in the knowing, in the awakened mind, we'd never be able to look at the mind. We'd be lost in confusion. So the refuge in knowing is very important. Together, the refuges are called the Three Jewels – and they are really like beautiful jewels that we can go back to whenever there is confusion, whenever there is agitation. We can always go back and take refuge in knowing those states. We don't have to think about them, we don't have to psychoanalyse ourselves. We can actually go back to the knowing. And what happens then is that we see what the Buddha saw: impermanence. We can see that these states are not worth holding onto because they are impermanent and not satisfactory. And we get the intriguing feeling that maybe we are not 'This.' Maybe it's got nothing to do with 'Me.' Maybe my depression is not 'My' depression.

Wouldn't it be wonderful to realize that one's sadness is actually not a personal thing? Because we tend to think that everything that happens to us is personal, we create many problems in our lives: 'Poor me, I'm the only one that this happens to. No one else has this problem, except me.' Everyone else looks terribly confident, don't they – especially if we lack confidence in ourselves. Everyone else seems to be terribly strong and seems to really know what he or she is doing. I used to think like that. I used to look at someone and, if I felt a bit depressed or miserable, I could be quite convinced that they were okay. They were fine. I was the only one who had problems until I realized they, too, had problems. Because we are self-centred creatures by nature, everything is 'my' problem, 'my' life, 'my' sorrows, 'my' relationships, and 'my' melodramas. Everything seems to centre around 'Me.'

Refuge in the Buddha allows us to see this very clearly. And it's a compassionate refuge. It's not a refuge that's critical. When we take refuge in mindfulness, we don't have to criticize or condemn or get angry with ourselves. We can observe the tendency to be critical, angry or demanding towards ourselves. This refuge in the Buddha is described in one of the first lines of our chanting as; 'the Buddha absolutely pure, with ocean-like compassion' and that's really what that refuge means. It is a beautiful, compassionate home.

So we have three homes, three refuges. We have refuge in the Buddha. It doesn't have a roof, no central heating, but it feels very good. It feels very secure, very reliable –

especially when you see how much of our life is so agitated, so unreliable and insecure. As we become more aware, we have a clear view and a clear understanding of what *saṃsāra* – the endless round of birth and death – is all about. And we are all here to get free from our attachment to it.

Much of our struggle in life is about trying to create situations where 'my' personality won't have to face suffering, or endure pain, won't feel embarrassed or ashamed. However every time we get lost or are unkind, angry, impatient or stupid, we can remember to be aware without judgement. We can acknowledge what is happening and accept it as it is. As soon as we have this clear vision of what's going on, we realize that our experiences are changing, and see clearly the uselessness of struggling to keep them permanent. We have to learn to be aware, to have mindfulness (*sati*) in our heart as a refuge that protects us, that protects the heart.

REFUGE IN THE DHAMMA

The second refuge, the Dhamma, is very close to the first one. In fact, there is a famous teaching that the Buddha gave to his disciples just before dying. They were anxious about him leaving this world and wondered who was going to be their teacher after the Buddha's passing away. They were concerned as to who was going to take over and be their guide. And he said: 'The Dhamma and the Vinaya will be your guide and your refuge.' On a previous occasion he had also said that: 'Who sees the Buddha sees the Dhamma, who sees the Dhamma sees the Buddha.'

Dhamma and Buddha – there's no need to have a physical Buddha. We can actually find the Buddha, the one who knows, the one who is aware, in our own heart. And as soon as we are aware, mindful, we are in touch with the Dhamma. That's the beauty of this practice.

Sometimes, when we read books about Buddhism, we think we have to read the whole *Tipiṭaka** before we can get in touch with the Dhamma. We believe that we have to learn the *Abhidhamma,*** perfect the ten pāramītas, develop the five spiritual faculties, get rid of the five spiritual hindrances and know the 56 states of consciousness, and so forth. By the end, we can feel so exhausted that we don't even want to start. In fact, today I was reflecting that when in our meditation period we mindfully breathe through our nostrils enduring a little bit of pain, a little bit of sweating or bearing with the heat and the cold, noisy people or boredom, we haven't got any idea of the amount of things we're really practising with. We don't know yet that at those moments we're perfecting the ten pāramītas, that we're letting go of the hindrances and developing the five spiritual faculties of faith, effort, mindfulness, concentration and wisdom. We might not be aware of it but we're really perfecting many spiritual qualities of the heart. But it doesn't seem like very much, does it? We're just breathing in through the nostrils and then breathing out, and then we feel a bit

---

Tipiṭaka: The Buddhist Pāli Canon.
**Abhidhamma*: A philosophical framework based on the Buddha's teachings.

of pain, then it's gone. Nothing much really. And yet over some years of practice we begin to see the fruits of our effort, and the teachings come alive.

So the refuge in the Dhamma is not something we have to look for very far. We don't have to look for the Dhamma somewhere out there, in another country, or in another person, or for a thing that will happen tomorrow or next year.

The quality of Dhamma is immediacy (*sandiṭṭhiko*) – right here, right now. It is timeless (*akāliko*). The Dhamma invites us to 'come and see' (*ehipassiko*), it leads inward (*opanayiko*) and can be realized when by oneself (*paccattaṃ veditabbo*) when awareness and wisdom are present. Each morning we chant those qualities. We don't have to wait for someone to tell us what it is. We don't have to read books or go through a progressive step-by-step study before we can get in touch with Dhamma.

The refuge in awareness brings us into the present and in the present we can see the Dhamma, the truth of the way things are. But this can only be seen when there is a clear awareness of the present moment, and a seeing of the nature of our mind and the way it functions. We can notice that it has its seasons and cycles, its time of darkness and brightness, its own rhythm. And because we are often unaware of this rhythm, we can sometimes drag ourselves to the point of complete exhaustion, sickness or stress and forget that we are part of nature, part of 'the way things are'.

Our intelligence, our capacity for knowledge, tends to alienate us from our nature. We often feel estranged from ourselves because our human nature is not really that exciting. Thoughts are so much more exciting! We can think, think, think the most wonderful things and the most miserable ones and our imagination can be quite creative, especially on retreat. We can really see how the mind is this wonderful creator. A famous Thai meditation teacher said once that in Buddhism it's not a God that creates, it's ignorance. We create out of ignorance. Sometimes we wonder what we have done in the past because our mind can think of the most bizarre things. We tend to have a lot of ideas of how things should be, how we would like things to be, how we think things should be, but have very little space for 'the way things are,' for what is happening in the moment as it is. In fact, after a while one can see a really clear pattern in the mind: there is what we think it should be, then there is what we'd like it to be, and finally what is. All three seem to have a bit of a hard time cooperating with each other. In my early years, it took me a while to notice this pattern but through the practice, I began to understand that in one moment we can only be aware of so much – which is often not very much. We can think a lot of things but we can actually know only a little. It's through knowing and investigating that which we are, that understanding deepens.

As long as we take things personally, we miss the Dhamma and are fooled by what arises in our mind. We fail to see that the things that we are taking personally are not what we are, nor what we think they are. We tend to believe and identify with the constant stream of thoughts, feelings and perceptions of our mind and it's no wonder that we become neurotic. It is a matter of practising with right attitude, with an attitude of compassion and infinite patience, rather than developing and perfecting any particular techniques. Because although we may have done a lot of practice and be an expert in breath meditation, body sweeping and all that, if we are still striving to develop the perfect *ānāpānasati* meditator our approach is wrong. Without a correct perspective, we are still caught up with the idea that we have to improve on 'Me.' The immediate and direct nature of the experience of Dhamma is something quite extraordinary. We can realize the nature of our thoughts without any intermediary, without interpretation, and see them just as they are. It is quite a remarkable thing and it's what attracted me most to this teaching. When I came to practice I was overjoyed at the simplicity and immediacy of the realization of the nature of the mind. You did not have to learn too much or get a Ph.D., you didn't have to start accumulating more knowledge. In the practice of Dhamma, there is a process of letting go, of emptying and freeing ourselves from the burden of knowledge, from the burden of accumulated experiences, from the heaviness of being somebody or carrying a person in the mind. I remember that when practising in the world as a layperson – now of course this is not to influence you all to become monks and nuns – I had the feeling that I was always 'somebody' practising. I found that very difficult. There was this burden of 'me' practising. When I came to the monastery I was ordinary and could forget about feeling 'special', some strange creature on the spiritual path, because everybody in the monastery was doing the same thing, you were just normal.

Much of our training in the monastery focuses on the ordinary. Daily, we spend periods of time cleaning, sweeping, dusting, walking from one room to the next, doing simple jobs and paying attention to the most mundane things such as opening doors, getting dressed, eating, getting up in the morning, brushing our teeth, putting our shoes on, going to the toilet, going to bed. Simple things like these are not exciting, and our mind learns to calm down and be more simple, more ordinary. We can see our mind wanting to make things special. If I had not been living in the monastery, I would never have seen the way the mind can create melodramas out of absolutely nothing. To be in touch with the ordinariness of our life is something very difficult for us because we have been conditioned to get our boost of energy through things that are interesting or stimulating. Or, we focus our attention on the next thing – on what's going to happen next.

Unless we have guidance and help from a wise teacher, from wise people who have an understanding of the path, we tend to carry on in our spiritual practice in the same way as before we started. We're still looking for fascination, for excitement, for something special, for the big bang, for the flashing lights, for the super insight that's going to solve all 'my' problems. I'm afraid it doesn't work like that. With the practice there is a change in our relationship with our mind. We let the flux of greed, hatred and delusion flow. We don't make a problem about it any more. We let the flow of our own mind just take its own course. We stop shaping the flux of our thoughts and feelings into this or that. Being in harmony with Dhamma is making peace with whatever is going on now, with 'the way things are', the Dhamma.

It's difficult to be ordinary and accept the triviality of our life. That's why most of the time we feel frustrated, because we think that somehow things are going to be different, or that they should be different, don't we? We sense that life shouldn't be just getting up in the morning, having breakfast, getting bored, having a cry with one's spouse, going to the toilet, eating, getting bored at work, coming back, watching television, going to bed, getting up in the morning, and on and on and on, day after day after day. We feel that somehow there must be something else. So we go on a trip and travel around the world – and we find out that even on the other side of the world, we still have to get up, we still have to go to the toilet, we still have to eat, we still get happy and bored with ourselves, we still get annoyed and depressed. We still get the same old 'me' – whether we are here, or in California, or in India, or anywhere. To come to terms with that has been the greatest teaching of monastic life.

Actually, monastic life is externally quite repetitive and boring. And if we identify with the structure or the routine then it's the most tedious lifestyle. It's so monotonous at times, you have no idea! But through accepting the perception and feeling of boredom for example, we realize that it's actually quite okay. It is not so much a matter of getting rid of boredom but of seeing what we are expecting from life.

I spent many years expecting from life something it could not give me. And in the same way if I expect something from the monastic life that it cannot give me, then I'll be very disappointed, frustrated or in a constant state of conflict.

So seeing the way things are is a very important realization because then we can actually work with life as it is, rather than expecting or dreaming about it. Expectations are like dreams. And most of our life is like a dream, or like a cloud, and we hope that this cloud will give us something real and substantial. Have you ever been able to shape a cloud? Or a dream? Yet this is what we are always trying to do isn't it?

So there's this dreamlike state that we create out of expectations, out of not understanding the limitations of our mind and body, of our life and the world we live in. But if we see those limitations for what they are, then a wonderful thing happens; we can actually work with life as it is. We don't have to expect something from it any more. We can actually give to our life. And that's a great change in the mind. Through the practice we begin to see that we don't have to ask or get or demand something from life. We can actually give, offer and joyfully respond to it. And this, we can all do.

The natural process of the realization of Dhamma is the awareness that life is a constant opportunity to give, to be generous, to be kind, to be of service in whatever situation we are in. As we let go we don't get so caught up and obsessed with ourselves. We can actually be useful. We can help. We can give. We can encourage ourselves and the people around us.

REFUGE IN THE SAṄGHA

The refuge in the Saṅgha, the last one, is the refuge in noble friendship – *kalyāṇamitta*. It symbolizes the community of men and women, ordained or living in the world, who have taken refuge in living wisely and compassionately, in accord with the Dhamma. They take refuge in harmlessness, loving-kindness and respect for all living beings. These are people who have a moral conscience. They are aware when they are acting foolishly or harmfully. This refuge symbolizes the purity of the human heart. I remember when for the first time I heard of the concept of the 'Pure Heart.' I thought that it was a beautiful expression and that's really what that refuge is; it's a refuge in that in us which is good, wholesome, compassionate and wise.

Before I started being interested in Buddhism, I used to do short retreats in Christian monasteries. The thing that struck me most in those places was this awesome, pervading feeling of respect for life and for each other. Even the silence seemed to be a kind of acknowledgement of reverence, of honouring the best in human beings. It was very moving. Even though I could not explain what it was, I sensed that people were devoted to something good and true. When I came to Chithurst and met the community for the first time, I had a very similar feeling of meeting human beings totally dedicated to honouring the truth, to being it and living in accordance with it.

And so the refuge in Saṅgha was the first thing that brought me to the monastic life.

My interest in joining the monastic Saṅgha came from the need to have a vehicle and a refuge of sanity in myself that would provide some guidance. I realized, for example, that without an ethical standard to contain and understand the energy of my desires, I was really in trouble. I was always very good at knowing what I should do, what I should be; I was a real expert at creating ideals! But somehow the energy of my desires had a very different agenda. My self-gratifying habits on the one hand and my yearning for truth on the other didn't meet, didn't seem to be very good friends.

One of the first things that became really clear when I joined the Saṅgha was that the precepts were my best friends and my best protectors. I never had the feeling that they were imposing themselves on me at all. On the contrary, I knew that they were supporting me and reminding me of being more mindful of my speech, my actions and my thoughts.

The training of our body and mind requires an enormous amount of patience and compassion. Our habits are strong and if we have lived a fairly heedless life in the past, we can't expect to turn instantly into a virtuous person. When we arrive at the monastery we don't become a saint overnight! And it is not a meditation retreat and the keeping of the precepts for ten days that is going to turn us into one either, is it? But at least we have a situation and a teaching that can help us to look at what is not correct or skilful in our behaviour and our habits. We learn to make peace and see them as they are. So we take refuge in the Saṅgha and use the standards followed by those who have walked the Path and liberated themselves before us. This refuge points to our commitment to virtuous conduct, to a way of life that protects and nurtures peace in the heart and reminds us of our intention to liberate it from ignorance. If we didn't have these guidelines, we would easily forget ourselves. And we are very good at that. In fact, that's what the mind is most intent on and does all the time, it forgets. But when we take refuge in mindfulness, in the Dhamma and in the purity of our intention to free ourselves from delusion, we remember that we have the necessary tools to train the heart. We can see clearly the unskilfulness of our habits, of our speech or of our thoughts and so on.

These refuges may appear as if they were three: Buddha, Dhamma, Sangha. But actually they are just one. We don't have one without the other. When there is virtue and the intention to live harmoniously, with compassion and respect for oneself and each other, then there's a naturally growing awareness, in harmony with the Dhamma, and we are more attuned to the truth. All of them interact and affect each other.

At first, we don't know quite what or where these refuges are. They may seem to be just words. You might even feel confused and have no trust in them. But as we practise, as we keep letting go of our attachments to thoughts, feelings, perceptions, they become a growing reality.

We can actually experience these refuges. They become a part of our life, a part of something that we can go back to, right here, right now. We don't have to wait. They are always present in our heart. Here, now, in the present. That's the real beauty of the practice of the Path. It's that total simplicity, that immediacy, complete in itself. There's nothing else that you need.

Just in taking the Three Refuges, you've got all the tools you need for your heart to be free.

10

ONE TIME …

Ajahn Candasiri

One time, after being very ill I began to think of things I would regret not having done. One of the things that came to mind was that if, on reaching the end of my life, I felt that I hadn't really enjoyed it that would be sad. If I hadn't really chosen how I lived, being driven instead by the spectre of Duty hovering in the background, that would feel unfortunate. It became clear to me that as a disciple of the Buddha my 'duty' is to be happy, to enjoy life; that being peaceful and at ease is, in fact, the fulfilment of his teachings – which were offered for our welfare and happiness. So I began to contemplate what it is that brings happiness, a sense of welfare and ease. Two things came to mind: firstly, recalling of the goodness of my life and, secondly, taking good care of myself.

I thought too that if I were to die with certain things

uncompleted that that also would be a pity. For example, I realized that it was important to express gratitude to the people who have really helped me in my life. So I wrote to them, acknowledging what they had done and what it had meant to me. Then I remembered others I had hurt, so I wrote to them too: 'Please forgive me for my insensitivity, the things I did that caused you unhappiness.'

It's important to set things straight because although it is absolutely certain that we will all die one day, we can never know how long we've got before that will happen. Now I don't intend to make you feel panicky or frightened; I just want to encourage you to take care of things as you go along. Don't put it off.

Consider: 'What would I regret not doing?' And then take steps to do it, whenever it's convenient. It may happen that circumstances don't allow you to attend to it straight away, or maybe it'll never be possible, but at least you've taken it on board, you've taken responsibility for your aspiration. I was delighted, talking with a friend of the community whom I hadn't seen for quite some time. He told me he had just been to Antarctica. I thought, 'Well, that's an unusual thing to do … ' but it was something that he had always wanted to do; so off he went – and had a wonderful time!

It's important to question, 'Is this okay?', 'Am I okay with this, have I really chosen to do this?' and if the answer is 'no', to ask, 'Is there something I can do to change it?' – rather than accumulating a kind of subliminal grudge or feeling of bitterness – that slightly sad, sour feeling that comes when we feel that we haven't really had any choice: 'It's all because of *them* that I had to do this!'

Sometimes we make assumptions about things we *have* to do or what *might* happen, without ever really questioning or considering: 'Will everything fall apart if I don't do this?' Or we may find that if we set up the right conditions to have a frank discussion with the person who's been driving us nuts, rather than continually procrastinating, that it's all right – in fact, quite a relief for all concerned!

I'm sure that everyone has a few conversations that are waiting to be had: conversations expressing appreciation, expressing tenderness or love. Perhaps we just assume that people know we love them, but have we actually told them? Or perhaps there are conversations that would be helpful: letting people know that things they are doing are really, really difficult for us. Can we attend to those? Or are we going to carry on allowing the irritation to gnaw away at us, draining away our sense of well-being year by year?

There is a phrase in the sharing of blessings chant: 'May the forces of delusion not take hold, nor weaken my resolve.' It is through these 'forces of delusion' that we allow ourselves to be undermined – those subtle, unwholesome thoughts and moods that can creep into consciousness. We may barely be aware of them but then, as soon as we notice them, we push them down – thinking that a good Buddhist must always be kind and loving; but why not try asking: 'What's going on here?' Allow those miserable little beings lurking there in the shadows to show themselves. Try listening to them, try showing them a little concern. You'll be amazed at the increased level of joy and energy in your life, as you begin to allow these things into consciousness. They only gnaw away as long as we don't pay attention to them. That's all they're asking for; once they've been heard they can go.

So we need to take stock, to ask: 'What's really important?', 'What do I want to do with my life?', 'Are there things I need to change?', 'Are there ways I can live more happily?' Or, 'Am I able, quite honestly and wholeheartedly, simply to rejoice in the way that my life is?' It may be that, for some of you, the answer is, 'Yes. I'm content with my relationships, my home situation, my work ... ' I really hope that that is the case for you – but if it's not, then it's good to consider ways to bring well-being and gladness into the heart.

If everything we do is from a sense of duty or a mild sense of bitterness or resentment, it's not going to bring a very happy result. The people we may be trying to help will pick up on it straight away; they'll feel that they're a burden, a nuisance. We don't want to make people feel like that, do we? It only really works when we've actually filled up our own heart with a sense of well-being – so it naturally pours out; rather than just wringing the last ounce of kindness out of a poor, parched little heart. Sometimes it feels like that, doesn't it? When it's like that we really need to take stock and think, 'What can I do to re-establish some sense of ease?'

Coming on retreat is something I would definitely recommend – regularly drenching your whole being with goodness; contemplating the teachings, recollecting what is wholesome, what upholds a sense of dignity and self-respect – then to consider how you can maintain this in your own life. For example, having a daily practice of recollection; meditating with others either in a monastery or in your own home; setting aside a day or half-day for a retreat in your own home; listening to tapes, reading Dhamma books – these are all things that can nourish the heart.

It's good too to use the Five Precepts as a structure for practice in daily life.

Generosity (*dāna*) is another extremely beneficial practice, giving according to our means either materially, or time, energy or attention. For example, we can cultivate the practice of listening, really being present for another person – this is an incredible act of generosity; taking ten minutes to really attend, to bear witness to their predicament – knowing that we are doing this as much for our own well being as for theirs. Our time, our interest and practical help – these count just as much as the more obvious practices of giving materially, in making the mind bright and joyous.

SOURCES OF TALKS

Ajahn Sundara's 'Freedom within Restraint', 'Simplicity' and 'Taking Refuge' have been taken from the collection of nuns' teachings, 'Freeing the Heart', which was first sponsored, edited and produced by Richard Smith in 2001. Similarly, the two talks, 'Why come to a Monastery' and, 'A Question of Balance' from Ajahn Candasiri both came from that same book. 'Fearless Presence' is a talk given by Ajahn Sundara at Seattle Insight in 2007 and 'The Knowing Mind' is a reflection offered on a ten day retreat she taught in 2009 at Amaravati. Ajahn Candasiri's offering 'Jesus through Buddhist eyes' is the transcript of a talk, given as part of the Radio 4 series, 'Jesus through many eyes' which was produced by Norman Winter. It is reprinted from 'Jesus in the World's Faiths: Leading thinkers from five religions reflect on his meaning', ed. Gregory A. Barker (New York: Orbis, 2008). 'Me First' is from a talk by Ajahn Candasiri that appeared originally in 'Awakening Presence' – a collection of nuns' teachings that was sponsored and put together by Sumi Shin. 'One Time …' is extracted from a talk she gave during a ten day retreat at Amaravati Retreat centre.